"Pat uncovers new insights into my father's life—his values, his faith, his intensely competitive spirit, and his serving heart."

Nan Wooden

"Pat Williams captures the essence of what makes John Wooden the greatest college basketball coach of all time. Coach Wooden was a Hall of Famer as a leader, mentor, and, most of all, in the game of life."

Dick Vitale—Hall of Fame college basketball analyst

"What a wonderful idea to capture Coach Wooden hard at work at his summer basketball camps. This book has great value to anyone in a position of leadership. I couldn't put it down."

Josh Pastner—Georgia Tech head men's basketball coach

"Pat Williams has given us another treasure trove of life lessons by the great John Wooden. This book provides valuable insights on how to be better in basketball and in the game of life."

Mike D'Antoni—Houston Rockets head coach

"Coach Wooden is an example for all of us to follow, and I have long held his words and philosophies in high regard. Pat Williams's new book about Coach Wooden will make a big difference in your life."

Michael Malone—Denver Nuggets head coach

"Pat Williams captures not only the greatness, but the goodness of John Robert Wooden. Other than my own father, Coach Wooden is the greatest man I've ever known. Williams's impeccable detail of this incredible teacher-coach provides a special treat for the reader. Enjoy it. He's given you a treasured seat right behind the bench of a Hall of Fame coach."

Dick Enberg—sportscaster, winner of multiple Hall of Fame and Emmy awards

"I got to meet Coach Wooden when I was a graduate assistant at the University of Kentucky after I played there. Coach Wooden would come to visit Kentucky after he had retired to watch practice. I had to pick him up at the airport and transport him back to the hotel. He was such a kind and gentle man. He had a presence about him that I will never forget. Pat has captured the essence of how Coach Wooden carried himself and the respect that he had throughout his coaching career. It is a great read. John Wooden represents all we should be as people and

 d coach

"Pat Williams' great new   rings it
all back—the fun, the exc   ketball

under the instruction of Coach John Wooden himself! It's impossible to measure his impact on the young people who passed through his camps, but through the stories Pat tells and through Coach Wooden's own words in this book, his much-needed influence continues to impact lives today."

Ann Meyers Drysdale—Retired basketball player,
WNBA executive, and sportscaster

"Pat Williams's book, *Success Is in the Details*, is terrific. Sometimes, we overthink ourselves as coaches when simple, character-driven principles are the most important things we can teach."

Dave Joerger—Sacramento Kings head coach

"One week at a John Wooden summer basketball camp changed the course of my life. The first day of camp, I dislocated a finger on an outdoor court rim, and Coach Wooden himself reset my finger. That was my introduction to Coach. He later recruited me to UCLA, where I had the honor of playing in four straight NCAA Final Fours. Pat Williams's new book captures the excitement and the life-changing impact the John Wooden camps had on me and countless other young people. A must-read for any Coach Wooden fan!"

Ralph Drollinger—President and founder of Capitol Ministries

"Once again, through his associations with Coach John Wooden, Pat Williams has captured the true man that Coach Wooden was. In *Success Is in the Details*, Williams has delved into Coach Wooden as a teacher in his youth camps, after his basketball coaching career at UCLA. Coach Wooden's systems and philosophies will continue to affect current and future generations to come. Pat Williams's book enforces Coach Wooden's legacy of teaching and communication that truly transcends time. This book will transform you."

Tubby Smith—University of Memphis head basketball coach

"I was fortunate to attend Coach Wooden's basketball camps, and be coached by John Wooden. The camps were a platform that helped me earn a basketball scholarship to UCLA, then play thirteen years of NBA basketball. Today, I continue to earn a living in the sport I love, and I give most of the credit to John Wooden. There was an aura around him that exuded greatness and evoked reverence—and Pat Williams has captured it in this book. I highly recommend it!"

Kiki VanDeWeghe—Vice President of Basketball Operations
for the NBA

SUCCESS IS IN THE DETAILS

SUCCESS IS IN THE DETAILS

and Other Life Lessons *from*
COACH WOODEN'S PLAYBOOK

PAT WILLIAMS
with Jim Denney

Revell
a division of Baker Publishing Group
Grand Rapids, Michigan

© 2018 by Pat Williams and James Denney

Published by Revell
a division of Baker Publishing Group
PO Box 6287, Grand Rapids, MI 49516-6287
www.revellbooks.com

Paperback edition published 2019
ISBN 978-0-8007-2739-0

Previously published under the title *Coach Wooden's Forgotten Teams*

Printed in the United States of America

The Library of Congress has cataloged the original edition as follows:
Names: Williams, Pat, 1940– author.
Title: Coach Wooden's forgotten teams : stories and lessons from John Wooden's
    summer basketball camps / Pat Williams, with Jim Denney.
Description: Grand Rapids : Revell, 2018. | Includes bibliographical references.
Identifiers: LCCN 2017036627 | ISBN 9780800726997 (cloth)
Subjects: LCSH: Wooden, John, 1910–2010—Anecdotes. | Basketball coaches—
    United States. | Basketball—Coaching. | Sports—Religious aspects—Christianity.
Classification: LCC GV884.W66 A3 2018 | DDC 796.323092 [B]—dc23
LC record available at https://lccn.loc.gov/2017036627

19 20 21 22 23 24 25   7 6 5 4 3 2 1

This book is gratefully dedicated to
Craig Impelman, Greg Hayes,
and Swen Nater.

Contents

Acknowledgments

With deep appreciation I acknowledge the support and guidance of the following people who helped make this book possible.

Special thanks to Alex Martins, Dan DeVos, and Rich DeVos of the Orlando Magic.

Hats off to my associate Andrew Herdliska; my proofreader, Ken Hussar; and my ace typist, Fran Thomas.

Thanks also to my writing partner, Jim Denney, for his superb contributions in shaping this manuscript.

Greg Hayes, author of *Camp with Coach Wooden: Shoes and Socks, The Pyramid,* and *"A Little Chap,"* was an amazing resource and encourager throughout the writing of this book. If you want to know more about how Coach Wooden impacted lives and taught basketball "the Wooden way," you *must* read Greg's book.

Craig Impelman shared his stories, insights, and profoundly helpful videos from the camps. He was generous beyond measure.

Swen Nater has long been a priceless resource whenever I have written about his friend Coach Wooden. He went above and beyond with this project and graciously granted permission to use his poems "A Week with Wooden" and "I Saw Love Once."

Hearty thanks also go to Andrea Doering, Alicia Cooper, and the entire Baker/Revell team for their vision and insight and for believing we had something important to say in these pages.

Finally, special thanks and appreciation go to my wife, Ruth, and to my wonderful and supportive family. They are truly the backbone of my life.

A Week with Wooden
by Swen Nater

His parents dropped him off
At the John Wooden basketball camp.
"Have fun son." And he draped his duffle bag
Over his right shoulder, turned and
Slowly walked toward the smiling faces
Of the cleanly dressed and friendly mannered
Men and women coaches behind the folding table.

A nice sociable lady said,
"This is your dorm number and room number,
And everything else you will need.
We're so glad you're here."
And she called him by name.

This camp was not going to be any different.
The faces, the food, the room, and the gym
Would be the same as the others.
But he didn't care; he just loved to play the game.

He threw his bag on his dorm room bed
And, with his well-worn basketball,
Headed down the hill and into the gym.
How he loved the dusty, musty air
And the rhythmic sound of bouncing basketballs.
As he stood, taking it all in,
A strong hand firmly folded over his left shoulder.

"I'm John Wooden and I'm so glad you came."
The boy turned and looked up into
Eyes that were kind but strong.

And through the week, those eyes
Winked when he did it right,
Stared when he failed and fell,
And scowled with a smirk
When he got full of himself.

That week with Wooden,
He learned the game of basketball,
But he also learned how to be an adult.

Used by permission.

Foreword

To the world, he was Coach John Wooden, the greatest coach of all time. To me, he was—and always will be—Daddy. And the same qualities that made him such a wonderful father also made him a great teacher and coach.

When Daddy was coaching at UCLA, my brother, Jim, and I loved going to the games. We'd sit in the stands with our mother, and before each game, Daddy and Mom would always perform a little ritual. He'd pull up his socks, then he'd reach over and tap his assistant coach on the knee. Finally, he'd turn and look at Mom up in the stands and make an okay sign with his thumb and forefinger—and the basketball game could begin.

That okay sign that passed between them was a tradition going back to their high school days, when Johnny Wooden was a star basketball player at Martinsville High in Indiana. Mom was the only girlfriend he ever had, the only girl he ever loved. They had met at a town carnival, but Daddy, being very shy, didn't know how to ask her out on a date. So at a Martinsville game, just before tip-off, he looked up into the stands and caught her eye. She was in the band, playing cornet, and when she saw him looking at her, she flashed him the okay sign, meaning, "Good luck!" And he gave the sign back to her, meaning, "Thanks!"

That was their secret code from then on. A game couldn't begin until their eyes met and he gave her the okay sign.

If only every child in the world could have parents like mine. When I was a child, I didn't realize what a rare privilege it was to be raised by parents of such loving, godly character. I had nothing to compare them to.

I not only grew up hearing all the wise, inspirational sayings you've read in Daddy's books (now known as "Woodenisms") but also had the privilege of watching him up close and knowing that he practiced every word he preached.

Daddy lived to serve people and to make others feel special. That's why he was never too busy for anyone. Whenever you spoke to him, he gave you his full attention. He listened. He was genuinely interested in you and everything you had to say. And when he spoke, whatever he told you was solid-gold wisdom you could apply to your life.

He had a deep love for my mother bordering on reverence. He thought she did everything perfectly, especially the way she took care of her home and her family. On one occasion, I found him on his knees in the kitchen with a towel. He was mopping up some spilled homemade orangeade from the floor—*then squeezing it back into the pitcher.*

Horrified, I asked him what he was doing.

He winked at me and said, "Don't worry, Nan—your mother's floor is so clean you can eat off it."

That was my Daddy, the wonderful, fascinating, one-in-a-million man you're about to discover (or rediscover) in these pages.

This is the fourth book Pat Williams has written about my father, John Wooden. With each new book, Pat seems to uncover some new facet of his character, some deeper understanding of what it was that made him so special.

Here Pat explores a time in my father's life that has long been neglected—Daddy's "second career" as a coach at summer youth basketball camps. Pat uncovers new insights into my father's life—his values, his faith, his intensely competitive spirit, and his serving heart. You'll encounter insights, stories, and words Daddy spoke that have never before been published. Pat also captures the essence of Dad's Pyramid of Success. The world is familiar with the Pyramid and the good character qualities it promotes. But I'm not sure everyone understands the *real* power of the Pyramid of Success.

Many people seem to think that the Pyramid was something my father taught his players *in addition* to teaching them the game of basketball. That's a misunderstanding. The Pyramid of Success was the foundation of everything he taught about basketball. It was the foundation of everything he taught about life. It was the foundation of the way he lived his life. It was the foundation of who he was as a husband, father, teacher, and man of God.

You can't understand his greatness as a coach until you understand his Pyramid. He formulated the Pyramid over a period of years—not so much as a set of lessons to teach but as a set of unbending principles he chose to live by throughout his life.

This is a book to be treasured, studied, and lived in. Whether you are a coach, an athlete, a sports fan, a business leader, a teacher—or you simply want to be a wiser, more influential human being—this book will deepen your understanding of the ideals and precepts that made Coach John Wooden the wonderful man he was.

So read on. Discover how my father impacted the lives of hundreds and hundreds of young people on those "forgotten teams" at his summer youth camps. Listen to his words. Rediscover his Pyramid. Imagine yourself as a boy or girl on a basketball court in the middle of summer, being taught by the greatest coach of all time. Then see how these stories and lessons change *your* life.

Nan Wooden
Los Angeles, California
January 15, 2017

Introduction

A Coach for All Seasons

Make greatness attainable by all.

Coach John Wooden

You and I could argue all day about who's the *second* greatest coach in the world. Phil Jackson? Don Shula? Mike Krzyzewski? Bear Bryant? Vince Lombardi? A good case could be made for any one of these great coaches.

But the greatest coach of *all* time in *any* sport? That's beyond dispute. Coach John Wooden has that position all sewn up. In July 2009, the *Sporting News* made it official by publishing a ranking of the fifty greatest coaches of all time, in every sport, both collegiate and professional. A blue-ribbon panel of sportswriters, coaches, and top athletes placed Wooden at the top. Over a twelve-year period, Coach Wooden's UCLA Bruins won an unparalleled ten NCAA national championships, including seven in a row. During that era, the Bruins won a record eighty-eight games in a row, not to mention two other winning streaks of forty-seven and forty-one games.

Before Coach Wooden arrived at UCLA, the school had never won a national championship and had won only two conference championships in the previous eighteen years. Coach Wooden achieved a dramatic turnaround in his first UCLA season, turning a 12-13 losing team into a 22-7 Pacific Coast Conference Southern Division champion. Coach Wooden's Bruins clinched the division title again the following year, this time with a 24-7 record. He established a tradition of sustained success throughout his tenure at UCLA.

Now, I've heard a few sports know-it-alls claim that Coach Wooden could never achieve such a feat in today's basketball environment. They spout such uninformed opinions as, "Anybody could win back-to-back championships with stars like Kareem Abdul-Jabbar and Bill Walton." Or, "There are more teams in the NCAA now—the competition would be much tougher." Or, "Coach Wooden taught an old-school approach that would never work today."

Well, that's a load of horsefeathers!

Greg Hayes has coached basketball at UCLA and the Master's College and is a color commentator for FOX Sports West. He's heard many of those same ignorant opinions, and he told me a story that broke my heart.

"A few years ago," Hayes said, "I was at UCLA to coach at a high school basketball camp that Jim Harrick ran. Jim had invited Coach to speak to the coaches at the camp. I was there with the other coaches, and I could hear some whispering and laughing. They were young, and they just didn't get who Coach was and what he'd accomplished. They just thought he was an old guy from back in the day and there was nothing they could learn from him.

"One guy was really disrespectful. I heard him say about Coach, 'He doesn't know anything anymore, so why are we here?' He must have thought Coach couldn't hear him, but I saw the look on Coach's face. He could feel the disrespect in the room. He was hurt. I saw it in his eyes. He was thinking, *Maybe I'm not relevant anymore. Maybe my time has passed.* Yet Coach was so humble and never complained when people criticized him.

"My heart went out to him. After his talk, the other coaches filed out, and I sat next to him. It was one of those moments when he was just so human. He was hurting, but he didn't say a word about it. We just talked. I wanted to let him know how much he meant to me. Just being there, sharing that moment, made me love him all the more.

"It also made me more determined than ever to let the world know that Coach is as relevant today as he ever was. I want people to know who Coach was and that his lessons are timeless. I want people to know that Coach Wooden was the greatest coach of all time and that if he was coaching today, he'd still be dominating everybody."

As I listened to Greg Hayes, I became angry thinking about those gym rats who thought they knew more about basketball than a man who was both a Hall of Fame player and a Hall of Fame coach (yes, John Wooden was inducted into the Hall of Fame *twice*). Hayes was right. John Wooden would still be winning championships if he was coaching today.

Coach Wooden won championships *with* superstar players and *without* superstar players. He won before Kareem and Bill Walton arrived, and he won after they left. He started building a winning tradition at UCLA when the basketball program was still housed in a decrepit, foul-smelling, Depression-era gymnasium known as the "B.O. Gym." UCLA's facilities were so embarrassingly bad that home games had to be played off campus at local high school gyms or at the Los Angeles Sports Arena.

During one basketball camp, Coach reminisced about his early days at UCLA, saying, "Under the conditions in which we worked, we had no home court, we practiced in a gym that only had two baskets, and the gymnastics team and the wrestling team were practicing right next to the basketball court. The gymnastics team had a lot of pretty coeds in leotards hopping up and down on trampolines, and I found it difficult to hold the attention of my players. I learned to accept those difficulties over which I had no control and to focus on the things I could control. We finally won our first championship, and we won under those exact conditions."

Is the competition tougher today than it was in Coach Wooden's day? Coach Ray Lokar, a leader in the Positive Coaching Alliance, spent a number of years coaching at Coach Wooden's camps. He explains why the competition was actually tougher during the Wooden era: "Back then you only got in the NCAA tournaments if you won your conference title. You had to be good for months to win the title back then. Now you can play poorly and struggle but get hot for a few weeks and win the title. . . . Do you know that Coach's ten NCAA title teams lost a total of ten games? And back then everyone was focused on beating UCLA, yet they still couldn't."[1]

> *"It's what you learn after you know it all that counts."*

Fact is, Coach was endlessly adaptable. When the game changed, he changed with it. Every year he focused on some aspect of the game and studied it intensely, often by interviewing other coaches. One of Coach's famous maxims was "It's what you learn after you know it all that counts." And he didn't just preach it—he lived it.

For example, in 1964, before UCLA had won its first national tournament, Coach Wooden was pondering how to play his undersized Bruins against significantly taller opponents. His assistant, Jerry Norman, suggested that UCLA's well-conditioned players and fast-paced offense would be more effective when paired with a zone press defense, designed to force opponents to make turnovers. Coach Wooden adopted Norman's suggestion—and UCLA's scoring surged. Instantly, the Bruins became a near-unstoppable force, with an undefeated record of 30-0, capping their season with a 98-83 victory over the taller-yet-slower Duke Blue Devils in the NCAA championship game. The UCLA zone press defense forced twenty-nine turnovers in that game and completely erased Duke's five-inch height advantage. That was the first of Coach Wooden's ten national championships.

No matter how the game has changed from Coach Wooden's time until today, or how much it might change in the future, Coach Wooden would have adapted. A commitment to continuous improvement was key to his character. Wooden was so much more than a product of his time. He was a coach for *all* times, a coach for *all* seasons.

I'm constantly amazed that I had the great privilege of knowing him and learning from him. Though I had followed Coach Wooden's career since his heyday at UCLA, my first personal encounter with him came in July 2000 when I checked my voice mail and heard him say, "Mr. Williams, this is John Wooden, the former basketball coach at UCLA." As if he needed any introduction.

He had called to offer his personal recommendation for a UCLA trainer who had recently applied to work for the Orlando Magic. He concluded, "Mr. Williams, I enjoy reading your books very much."

I had to sit back and absorb the fact that the legendary Coach John Wooden had called and wanted to talk to *me*. Then I returned the call, and we had a wonderful chat. He spoke as if we were old friends. That was the first of many encounters I would have with Coach Wooden over the next decade, until he passed away in June 2010. During the final decade of his life, he invited me into his life in an amazing way.

Whenever I was on the West Coast, I would make a pilgrimage to Coach Wooden's modest, middle-class condo in Encino, California. At five o'clock sharp, we'd get in my rental car and head

23

to Sherman Oaks for dinner at the Valley Inn, Coach Wooden's favorite dining spot. We'd arrive in time for the early bird special and the Valley Inn's famous clam chowder. We'd talk about our shared love of basketball, our shared faith, and our shared fascination with history. The more I learned from him, the more I wanted to write about this great man and all the things he taught me. So I approached Coach Wooden for permission to write a book about his life and success principles. He gave me his humble permission: "Though I'm not worthy of a project like this, if you would like to write this book, you go right ahead." So in 2006, my first book about Coach was published: *How to Be Like Coach Wooden.*

I thought that book said all there was to say about Coach, but as I continued talking to him and the people who knew him, I discovered I had barely scratched the surface of this man's wisdom and greatness. I learned that his life had been shaped by a simple seven-point philosophy that his father had taught him, so I journeyed to Indiana, to the town where John Wooden grew up and the farm where he was born. Then I wrote *Coach Wooden: The 7 Principles that Shaped His Life and Will Change Yours.*

In 2014, I wrote a book about an insight Coach Wooden had shared with me over dinner at the Valley Inn—*Coach Wooden's Greatest Secret: The Power of a Lot of Little Things Done Well.* Once again, I thought I had plumbed the depths of this man's deep wisdom. And once again, I was wrong.

Soon after that book was published, I heard about the John Wooden Basketball Fundamentals Camp, which he conducted from 1971 (while he was still coaching at UCLA) to the mid-1980s. Most people thought that after Coach had retired from college basketball coaching in 1975, he had faded into obscurity. But Coach had not gone fishing. He had moved on to a new phase of his career as a teacher, mentor, and coach. Every summer he led three weeklong basketball camps, each camp accommodating approximately three hundred campers. Instead of being Coach to a dozen college basketball players each year, he was Coach to nine hundred basketball campers ranging from elementary-

"Make greatness attainable by all."

school age to high-school age. Many of his camps included both boys and girls. Coach was living out his own maxim "Make greatness attainable by all."

You can't go to a John Wooden Basketball Fundamentals Camp. But through these pages, I'm going to take you back in time. I'm going to help you experience what it was like to be coached by the greatest coach of all time.

So put on your gym socks and lace up your shoes. Grab a basketball and meet me in the gym. Let me introduce you to my friend, my mentor, my coach—John Wooden.

Pat Williams
Orlando, Florida

25

1

More than
a Basketball Camp

Seek opportunities to show you care. The smallest gestures often make the biggest difference.

Coach John Wooden

Craig Impelman was an assistant men's basketball coach at UCLA
in the post-Wooden era, 1976 to 1984. In 1984, he married Coach
Wooden's granddaughter Christy and became part of the family. Impelman conducted his own basketball camps, and Coach
Wooden spoke at those camps for a number of years.

Impelman would sometimes introduce Coach Wooden to his
campers with this story: "I was a fan of John Wooden for years.
I was an assistant coach at UCLA, and I wanted to become as
much like Coach Wooden as I could. While at UCLA, I often
visited Coach Wooden at his home and talked basketball. He was
the greatest basketball coach around, and I thought I knew him
pretty well.

"One year I attended a basketball camp in Santa Barbara where Coach Wooden was speaking. While I was sitting in the bleachers, waiting for him to speak, I said to a coach sitting next to me, 'You know, the greatest thing about Coach Wooden is that he's an even better person than he is a basketball coach.'

"Sitting in front of me was a man named Max Shapiro, who had run Coach Wooden's basketball camps for years. Max overheard me, and he turned and said, 'Craig, you're missing the whole point about Coach Wooden. The reason he's such a great basketball coach is *because* he's such a great person.'

"Max opened my eyes. I finally understood what I should have known all along: being a good person is essential to being successful in life. You've got to be a good person *first* before you can even think about being a great coach or a great basketball player. Coach Wooden won ten national championships during his last twelve years coaching at UCLA. The most national championships any other school has won? Three.

"But here's the amazing thing: that's the accomplishment Coach Wooden is the *least* proud of! He'll tell you he's more proud of the fact that his players all graduated and went on to become doctors, lawyers, and ministers. He's more proud that the people he taught went on to become good people who did good things in life. So if you get anything out of this week at camp, I hope you learn how to be a good person like Coach Wooden."

Impelman's introduction helped set the tone for the entire week at camp. The most important goal of Coach Wooden's basketball camps was building character.

Max Shapiro—the man who ran Coach Wooden's camps—is a longtime friend of mine. While researching this book, I called him and asked him how the John Wooden Basketball Fundamentals Camp began.

"In 1970," Shapiro said, "I was living in San Diego. I drove up to UCLA to meet with Coach Wooden. At that point, he was making $25,000 a year coaching the Bruins. I said, 'Coach, I'd love to do summer camps with you. We could do them at California Lutheran University in Thousand Oaks. We could hold three week-long camps for three hundred kids per week. That would be nine hundred campers each summer. I would pay you forty dollars per camper for a total of $36,000 for the summer. What do you think?'

"Coach replied, 'Max, I appreciate your interest, but I must decline. I have to be at school, and it's an hour's drive from the campus to Thousand Oaks, and I don't like to drive.'

"I said, 'Coach, we can solve that. I'll have a driver for you every day, and we'll work the schedule out so you can be back at school by three in the afternoon.'

"Coach said, 'Okay, let's try it.'

"So we held our first camp at Cal Lutheran in the summer of 1971. Eventually, those summer camps put all of his grandkids through college."

The Living Legacy of the Camps

Actor Jim Caviezel played the demanding title role in Mel Gibson's *The Passion of the Christ* and starred in the CBS crime drama *Person of Interest* for five seasons. Caviezel's father, James Sr., played freshman basketball at UCLA under Coach Wooden and assistant Jerry Norman in 1959–60. The senior Caviezel likely would have played on Coach Wooden's first championship team if a knee injury hadn't cut short his playing career.

Despite that injury, Jim Caviezel's father maintained a lifelong friendship with Coach Wooden and made sure that his son attended Coach Wooden's summer basketball camps. "I knew Coach Wooden until he died," the younger Caviezel recalled. "He'd come over, and he was like my grandfather. . . . I watched him and was connected to him through my entire life."

Jim remembered his father giving him a choice: either go to Coach Wooden's basketball camp or work on a farm baling hay. It was a no-brainer—Caviezel went to camp. There he learned the fundamentals of the game—and the fundamentals of life, as taught through the Pyramid of Success.

Caviezel observed that Bruins fans "won't be surprised to know the first thing Dad ever taught me was to put my socks and shoes on properly. Coach Wooden told his players that wrinkles cause blisters and blisters steal time. He said getting socks and shoes right was the start of everything they'd need to know for the rest of their lives. . . . Attending Coach Wooden's summer basketball camps, I learned to stay in my game, focus on execution, and ignore the scoreboard."

Through the Pyramid of Success, Coach Wooden taught young Jim Caviezel the importance of maintaining one's character and values. A devout Catholic, Caviezel rejects any screen roles that would violate his faith. Though Caviezel works in an industry dominated by narcissistic egos, he is known for his humility and strong moral principles. He is a walking testament to the positive influence of Coach John Wooden.[1]

Greg Hayes attended his first John Wooden basketball camp immediately after his graduation from UCLA in 1977. That first year he served as a camp counselor. He returned every summer for the next twelve years as a coach. Hayes told me, "Coach Wooden influenced hundreds of players during his twenty-seven years of coaching, but in the summer basketball camps, he influenced well over ten thousand campers and probably more than a thousand coaches, including me.

"His camp coaches went on to great things because of what they learned directly from Coach. And there were many indirect benefits of coaching at his camps as well. Just being associated with Coach Wooden opened many career doors for us. The coaches learned from each other, and many of the older coaches mentored the younger ones. Coach Wooden made sure that only the most highly motivated coaches worked at his camps.

"We made friends and contacts that were helpful in our careers. And Coach himself was always willing to make phone calls and write letters to help us find jobs. Many camp coaches were high school, community college, and college coaches. We all became better classroom teachers as well as better coaches because of Coach Wooden's influence.

"The camps were run efficiently and professionally. But the important thing was that so many lives were touched. We were like family. We cared for each other. There was very little turnover from year to year. Most of the staff returned every summer.

"One way the influence of Coach Wooden's camps has continued is through the coaches who have gone on to run their own camps. They use their basketball camps the same way Coach Wooden used his—to teach character and life skills. Coach set an example that people want to follow. His influence goes on and on. That's the legacy of his camps."

Day One: Sunday

The camps opened early Sunday afternoon. Most years Coach Wooden and his wife, Nell, came straight from church, and she assisted with the check-in and registration of the campers. Coach and Nell often brought their granddaughters to help, and Greg Hayes recalled, "All the counselors and young coaches were in love with their granddaughters."

Campers and staff were abuzz with excitement on opening day. Some were about to experience their first Coach Wooden camp. Others were returning for the second or third time. All were excited about being in the presence of the greatest coach of all time.

Some coaches came from across the country, but most were top coaches from local high schools, colleges, and community colleges. They didn't come only to teach. They came to *learn*. The coaches saw the camps as a chance to recharge their own batteries while improving their coaching and teaching skills.

Coaches arrived by 1:00 p.m. and gathered for their first meeting with Coach Wooden at 2:30—a coaches' clinic that set the tone for the week. The coaches' handbook summed up Coach Wooden's expectations for his staff: "A great deal of the camp's success will be due to the enthusiasm, willingness, and cooperation of you, the *coach*. It is imperative that you are at your best at all times during the week."

Next, Coach Wooden spoke at a meeting of parents and campers to set forth goals and expectations. Then Coach led the campers in an exercise that went back to his earliest days as a college coach: showing his players how to put on their socks and shoes. At first glance, this might seem like an extreme case of majoring in the minors. These kids had come to learn the UCLA high post offense and the zone press defense. Why was Coach teaching them how to put on their socks and shoes?

Knowing how to properly care for one's feet was foundational to everything Coach Wooden wanted to teach his campers—and not merely because he was concerned about blisters. I think Coach was teaching his players a lesson in character and humility.

It's a humbling thing to be told how to put on your socks and how to tie your shoes. These are skills we all learn before entering kindergarten. If his lesson was simply about blisters, Coach could have addressed it in a printed handout. But I think Coach was teaching much more than proper foot care. He was teaching his players the importance of small details in every aspect of the game, in every aspect of life. He was teaching the character trait of humility. He was teaching the importance of following instructions.

I recently talked to Steve Kerr, who played for the Bulls, Spurs, and Trail Blazers in the NBA and now coaches the Golden State Warriors. I asked him about the John Wooden basketball camps, and his eyes lit up. "Oh yeah, absolutely," Kerr said with a grin. "I went to Coach Wooden's summer camp for two years. I remember the first thing Coach Wooden taught us was how to put on our socks and shoes and to make sure our room keys were attached to our sneaker laces and tied tight so we wouldn't lose our room keys. He taught us all the UCLA basketball drills, but the socks, shoes, and room keys were the first order of business. Boy, those were fun days."

Entrepreneur Dick Kazan recalled taking his twelve-year-old son, Kyle, to a John Wooden camp in 1979. "I recall a hot summer day and a packed gym," he said. "The kids were laughing and shouting out to one another as basketballs bounced on hardwood flooring, the noise echoing to the rafters. . . . Then everything fell silent as the word spread, *Coach Wooden is coming*. And with no fanfare, this man of such quiet but powerful presence walked into the room."[2]

Sunday was also the day the three hundred campers were divided into thirty-two teams, and the teams were divided into associations or conferences. The teams were formed largely on the basis of a random drawing but with some redistribution of players if it seemed that some teams had too much or too little talent.

After dinner, campers enjoyed free time until 8:15 p.m., when they reported to the gym for roll call. In the gym, the campers watched UCLA championship game films. Then at 9:30, the campers all headed to their dorm rooms. They were allowed a phone call home, a shower, and time to unpack before lights out at 10:00 p.m.

Dormitory roommates were usually assigned by random drawing. One lesson campers were expected to learn was how to make new friends and get along with others.

Day Two: Monday

Monday was the first full day of the camp. A driver (usually a counselor) brought Coach to the camp. He generally arrived at 6:30 or so in the morning to have breakfast in the cafeteria with the campers and coaches at 7:00. At 8:00, everyone—campers, counselors, coaches, support staff, and Coach Wooden himself—gathered for a group camp photo. The coaches reminded the campers that all shirts had to be tucked in.

After the photo session came the basketball drills. Coach taught the first half hour of drills himself. The camp had his name on it, and he made it special. He was fully involved in each camp, and that's why his campers and coaches kept coming back summer after summer.

The first half hour was intensive. Coach put his campers through the same drills he used to teach his championship teams at UCLA. Coach wanted to create the same culture in his camps that he had produced in his UCLA teams—a culture of mutual respect and consideration, of discipline and hard work combined with enthusiasm, a culture that focused on executing the fundamentals.

I recently had lunch with Basketball Hall of Famer Jamaal "Silk" Wilkes, who was a key player with Coach Wooden's Bruins before going on to a stellar NBA career with the Golden State Warriors and the Los Angeles Lakers. Wilkes was a frequent guest speaker at Wooden's basketball camps, and he told me he was impressed with the way Coach ran the camps. "Coach was very engaged with the campers," Wilkes said, "very hands-on. He took great pride in the caliber of instruction offered at the camps. It was UCLA-level instruction. Coach always saw himself as a teacher and was never concerned about self-promotion or acting like a big shot. He always represented UCLA and his own code of ethics the best he could in everything he did. And that included the summer basketball camps."

During the morning drills, Coach Wooden paced the stage and used a microphone to call out encouragement, instructions, and his signature maxims: "Flexibility is the key to stability" and "Be quick but don't hurry." He observed each player and sometimes directed one of his coaches to work with a player on technique. Campers were often surprised that this soft-spoken, grandfatherly man could be as authoritative as a Marine Corps drill sergeant. Coach was positive and encouraging, but when he blew his whistle, campers instantly gave him their attention. Coach was one of those rare individuals who commanded with authority but without fear.

"Flexibility is the key to stability."

Coach ended every workout just as he ended his UCLA practices. He always concluded with a word of approval or a joke. His habit of ending workouts on a positive note reflected his belief that teachers should always encourage and affirm—that's the best way to get a lesson across to students.

Next, campers rotated through eight skill stations, each station focused on a specific skill: dribbling, passing, shooting, lay-ups, pick-and-rolls, stops and pivots, rebounding and defense, and the elements of the UCLA high post offense. These were the same drills Coach Wooden used with his UCLA players during the championship seasons.

While his coaches conducted the eight-station drills, Coach Wooden took a five- or six-mile walk around the campus accompanied by a camp director or counselor. Greg Hayes and Max Shapiro both mentioned a habit Coach displayed on those walks: if there was any litter along the way, even a gum wrapper, he'd go out of his way to pick it up and dispose of it. Shapiro recalled, "We'd be walking along the grounds at Cal Lutheran, and if Coach saw a piece of paper twenty feet away, he'd go over and pick it up." When Coach Wooden stooped to pick up trash, he made an impression on coaches, counselors, and campers. He showed by example the kind of person he wanted them all to be.

Coach returned from his walk before lunchtime. And lunchtime was work time for Coach. He sat at a table surrounded by coaches, and they asked him questions and sought his advice. This was an informal coaches' clinic over cafeteria food. Many coaches reported that those meals with Coach Wooden were some of the most instructive and memorable times of their camp experience.

Though some of Coach Wooden's camps were held at places like Point Loma Nazarene University in San Diego or Pepperdine University in Malibu, most of the Wooden camps were held at California Lutheran University in Thousand Oaks, California. Throughout the 1970s and the 1980s, Coach Wooden's camps shared the Cal Lutheran campus with the Dallas Cowboys, who used the university's football facilities for their training camps. As a result, two coaching legends often had lunch in the same dining hall at the same time: John Wooden and Tom Landry.

During lunchtimes with Coach, Greg Hayes listened to conversations Coach Wooden had with his basketball camp coaches—and he took careful notes. In those notes, he preserved reams of coaching wisdom so that it could be shared with the world. For example, during one of those lunches, a coach asked how to coach an underachiever.

"All of us are underachievers," Coach Wooden replied. "There is no such thing as an overachiever."

"All of us are underachievers," Coach Wooden replied. "There is no such thing as an overachiever."[3] Coach went on to explain that we all have the capacity to achieve great things. If we are making the effort to do the best of which we are capable, we will achieve 100 percent of our capacity, and we can be at peace with ourselves. We sometimes hear about coaches who demand "110 percent" from their players, but there's no such thing. As leaders and coaches, we should not expect more of our people then 100 percent—but we should always ask them to give the best of which they are capable. At 1:00 p.m., right after lunch, campers assembled in the gym for a half-hour workout with Coach, followed by a ninety-minute workout with their own coaches. Campers quickly learned they should eat a light lunch—or pay the price of overindulgence during the fast-paced afternoon practice.

The afternoon practice focused on the fundamentals of the UCLA high post offense—the offensive strategy that Coach Wooden implemented with unprecedented success at UCLA. It was a flexible man-to-man offense that involved the abilities of all five players on the floor, emphasizing unselfishness, passing, and teamwork. Elements of the high post offense are now in use throughout college and professional basketball, yet the fundamentals of the strategy were simple enough that Coach could teach them to his youngest campers. Players needed to learn the offense before the start of official games on Wednesday.

Day Three: Tuesday

On Tuesday, Coach Wooden gave his Pyramid of Success talk to the campers (in chapter 4, we'll see how Coach made this life-changing message come alive for these young people). Coach also brought in guest speakers, including some of his past players, to teach the campers about basketball and life.

During the morning and afternoon drills (and later in the week, during the games), Coach walked around, both inside and outside the gym, making suggestions to coaches, giving pointers to individual players, and calling out encouragement.

Each day in the midafternoon, a camp staff member (usually a counselor) drove Coach home to his condo in time for dinner. The assignment of driving Coach to and from the camp became a sought-after privilege. It was a distinct honor to serve as Coach's driver for the day. While driving Coach, a driver got to spend one-on-one time with Coach—asking questions, listening to stories, and soaking up wisdom from a coaching legend. Some of Coach Wooden's drivers asked permission to run a tape recorder during the drive, and Coach was always happy to oblige.

Imagine being able to have wide-ranging conversations with Coach about anything from basketball strategy to living by faith. Some of Coach's drivers were almost paralyzed with nervousness at the thought of having this living legend in their car. One driver recalled driving fifty-five miles an hour in the slow lane, keeping his hands at the ten and two o'clock positions on the steering wheel. But no matter how awed or nervous a driver might be, Coach sat back, relaxed, conversed, and never said a critical word about his chauffeur's driving—and Coach managed to put most of them at ease. He never seemed to mind that many of his young chauffeurs transported him along the crowded freeway in aging clunkers, often with poor brakes and no air-conditioning in the summer heat.

Meanwhile, back at the camp, the coaches put their campers through afternoon practice sessions. Then, after the last practice, campers had free time until dinner at 4:30. During free time, some campers chose to go swimming. Others, feeling exhausted, dragged themselves back to the dorms for a nap. Many campers took part in optional afternoon skill clinics the coaches ran from 3:10 to 4:10 on Monday and Tuesday. Others played pickup games in the gym or worked on their shooting on the outdoor courts. Most of the campers were there to play basketball, and that's what they did—every chance they got.

Days Four and Five: Wednesday and Thursday

On Wednesday, the games began. On that day, the camp experience took on a whole new dimension. Enough practice, enough drills.

It was finally time to compete! Though drilling and teaching were Coach Wooden's favorite parts of the camps, for the campers, it was all about the competition.

The games were refereed by the counselors, and each game was forty minutes long, consisting of two twenty-minute halves. Each team was required to run the UCLA high post offense they had practiced on Monday and Tuesday. Coach Wooden expected the games to be instructive as well as fun. He also expected players to demonstrate good sportsmanship in the UCLA tradition.

Coach Wooden wanted his campers to learn authentic organized team basketball. The handbook for coaches demanded that coaches set an example for their players: "The purpose of the competition is to allow campers an opportunity to put into practice what they are learning throughout the day and to learn to play together on a team. Winning at the cost of swearing, losing your temper, or otherwise setting a poor example for your players will not be tolerated!"[4]

The John Wooden Basketball Fundamentals Camp employed an ingenious system of substitutions to ensure that all campers enjoyed equal playing time, while making sure the teams were highly competitive. Each player was assigned a number, and a team's two best players were given special numbers in the system to ensure that at least one of them was on the floor at all times. Making sure that every player got equal playing time helped equalize differences in talent between teams so that there were fewer lopsided matchups. It also ensured fair treatment for all campers, from the most to the least talented.

Greg Hayes said there's a legend that the substitution system was developed as a counterweight to an intense competition between two camp coaches. In the early days of the camps, two coaches were so focused on beating each other that they overplayed their best players, while the less-gifted players warmed the bench. A displeased Coach Wooden pointed out that his camps were about teaching, not winning. All campers deserved equal playing time. So the coaches developed the substitution system to correct the imbalance.

The Wooden camps exposed young players to a spectrum of coaching styles and personalities, under the auspices of Coach himself. Some of the camp coaches were loud, passionate, and emotional. Others were quiet, analytical, and reserved. Not only was the mix of personalities and coaching styles valuable for the campers, but the coaches also benefited from watching one another, talking to one another, and learning from one another.

Games were played all day Wednesday and all day Thursday on the indoor court in the gym and on the outdoor courts. The games culminated in a championship game on Thursday afternoon. Thirty-two teams competed, but only one could win the ultimate prize—the camp championship trophy.

Day Six: Friday, the Final Day

Friday began with a hearty breakfast. Over scrambled eggs and sausages, campers talked excitedly about the emotional high of the previous day's championship game. Some campers were somber, knowing that this glorious week of instruction, inspiration, and competition was coming to an end. After breakfast, the coaches took the players through one last set of drills. Then the campers assembled for an awards ceremony.

Todd Wasserman, who now works in the motion picture industry, attended Wooden's camps at Cal Lutheran. "In the summer of 1984," he told me, "I was nine years old. I went with a friend to the Wooden camp. The first few days I was miserable and homesick. The players were divided into teams, and I started the week as the most timid and fearful player on my team, but the coaches were great. They really encouraged me during the week.

"On Friday, they presented an award to one kid on each team. The coaches and counselors selected one camper to receive the camper of the week award. The winner got the Coach Wooden Pyramid of Success mounted on a plaque. And guess what? I got the camper of the week award on my team. It's an award for the camper who demonstrates a coachable attitude, strong work ethic, cooperation, team spirit, good listening, and so forth. I think the coaches felt I had grown the most during the week. I still have that plaque, and to this day, I look at it for inspiration.

"When I see that award, I think, *Here I am in my mid-forties, and if those coaches saw these attributes in me when I was nine, I must still have these attributes today.* And that thought keeps me motivated. I keep believing that I have the attributes Coach Wooden taught in the Pyramid, and I'm committed to going deeper and deeper into those attributes every day.

"In the movie industry, it's easy to get discouraged. I write a script, knowing that it may never get accepted, may never see the light of day. But I keep Coach Wooden's definition of success before me, and I have peace of mind in knowing I made the effort to do the best of which I'm capable. If I've truly done my best, I'm a success. Coach Wooden's philosophy of success has had a lasting effect on me, and I'll never forget that awards ceremony at the end of the week."

Coach Wooden closed the awards ceremony with a talk and a poem. Here's an example of one of Coach Wooden's closing talks, transcribed from a videotape Craig Impelman shared with me.

"When I graduated from the eighth grade," Coach said, "my father gave me two things: a two-dollar bill and a piece of paper on which he had written a seven-point creed—seven pieces of advice. He said, 'As long as you keep this two-dollar bill, you'll never be broke. I still have that two-dollar bill to this day. And he said, 'Try to live up to this seven-point creed, son, and you'll never go wrong.' I kept that creed in my wallet until the paper became almost unreadable.

"The first point of that creed is 'Be true to yourself.' If you are true to your principles, if you choose to do the right thing at all times, then you'll be true to everyone else.

"The second point is 'Help others.' Show love for your fellow man. When you help others, you help yourself even more.

"The third point is 'Make each day your masterpiece.' Do the best you can every day. You can never make up for a wasted day.

"The fourth point is 'Make friendship a fine art.' Don't forget the friends you've made this week at camp. Goodness gracious, no. Keep in contact with them after this week is over.

"The fifth point is 'Drink deeply from good books.' Not just trash or popular novels, but good books. And it's wise to turn to the Greatest Book every day.

"The sixth point is 'Build a shelter against a rainy day.' Think about the future, not just today. Save your money. Help others and let them help you. Keep learning new things every day. Then when a rainy day comes, you'll have saved up some money, some friendships, and some wisdom to see you through. Someone wisely said, 'Live as if you're going to die tomorrow, and learn as if you're going to live forever.'

"The seventh point is 'Give thanks for your blessings.' Be thankful to the Lord for the good things you have, and ask him for help and guidance.

"My father gave me that seven-point creed when I was thirteen, and I have tried to live by it. I wish I could say I lived it perfectly. I can't, but I do try. That's the important part.

"Now, coaches and counselors and older campers, I hope you'll always set a good example for the young people. Our young people need role models. They need to follow good role models. They need role models more than they need critics. They need to learn not only the right way to play basketball but the right way to live their lives. Some of the people playing professional basketball today, they're not good role models at all. So it's up to you older ones to set a good example for the younger ones to follow.

"And young people, be careful and selective about the people you choose as your heroes. Make sure that the people you follow, the people you listen to, are wise people who set a good example. Make sure they are truly heroes, and they have earned the right to be role models.

> *"Our young people ... need role models more than they need critics."*

"When my son was born, I was doing some work for a book publishing company. I taught English in high school for many years and did a lot of editing work in addition to my teaching job. It helped to pay the bills. And this publishing company not only sent me a check for my work but also sent me a set of encyclopedias called *The Book of Knowledge*. And included with the encyclopedias was a poster that showed a man walking along the seashore with his son right behind him. The boy was following his father's footsteps in the sand and trying to walk exactly where his father walked.

"This picture is about the example we all set for others. As parents, teachers, coaches, and basketball players, we set an example. People are following us and watching our example, whether we realize it or not. That's the message of this poster. There was a poem printed next to the picture of the father and his son, and I memorized that poem. It read:

A careful man I must always be;
A little fellow follows me.
I know I dare not go astray,
For fear he'll go the self-same way.

I cannot once escape his eyes;
Whate'er he sees me do, he tries.

Like me, he says, he's going to be,
This little chap who follows me.

He thinks that I am good and fine,
Believes in every word of mine.
The base in me he must not see,
This little chap who follows me.

I must be careful as I go,
Through summer sun and winter snow,
Because I am building, for the years to be,
This little chap who follows me."

Coach Wooden recited that poem by an anonymous author at the end of every camp just before noontime. That poem signaled the end of Coach Wooden's last talk of the week—and the end of the camp.

Max Shapiro told me he loved the moment when Coach Wooden finished reciting that poem and said farewell to the campers. "That was the highlight of the Wooden camps for me," he said. "The basketball drills were over. All the awards had been presented. All the talks had been given. All the photos had been taken. This whole exciting experience had come to an end. At that moment, without any prodding, all these young campers would rise up as one and give Coach a spontaneous standing ovation. You can't fool kids. Their loving response to Coach came from the heart. During the week, they had come to know him and love him. They had gotten to know who he was and what he had just added to their lives. They couldn't thank him enough."

The sports world remembers Coach John Wooden for the legendary string of championships his teams won in the final dozen years of his coaching career. He created a college basketball dynasty that will probably never be equaled. Yet Coach himself shrugged off his legendary accomplishments as if they didn't matter. All that mattered to him was that he had been a faithful teacher who had

44

impacted young lives. And by that standard, he was even more successful in his retirement than he had been while coaching at UCLA.

The thousands of campers who passed through the John Wooden Basketball Fundamentals Camp from 1971 to the mid-1980s all knew that they were in the presence of greatness—not greatness as measured by sportswriters and sports fans but greatness as measured by John Wooden's depth of character and breadth of love. As a coach, as a leader, as a teacher, as a mentor, and as a man of faith, Coach John Wooden was not merely a rarity. He was absolutely unique, incomparable, one of a kind. That's why, year after year, camp after camp, the young people he influenced rose up as one and gave him a standing ovation. No ovation was ever more fitting or more honestly earned.

Coach Wooden influenced generations with authentic love. And that's why he received so much love in return.

2

Success Is in the Details

It's the little details that are vital. Little things
make big things happen.

Coach John Wooden

Kurt Helin, managing editor of ProBasketballTalk.com (the NBA
blog of NBC Sports), recalled attending the John Wooden Basketball Fundamentals Camp when he was "a skinny little fourth-
grader growing up in Los Angeles." He was excited about being
at Coach Wooden's camp, and he wanted to show off his jump
shot for "the coach who didn't lose."

The first day of camp made a huge impression on Helin. He
was in the gym with all the other campers—and in walked Coach
Wooden. It was a scene, Helin said, totally unlike many basketball
camps today where a basketball celebrity "walks in on the last day,
gives a speech, shakes some hands, takes his check, and moves on.
Wooden was there, hands-on, every day."

According to Helin, Coach Wooden started the camp exactly as he had started each season as coach of the UCLA Bruins: "He told us to sit down and take off our shoes and socks." Helin never forgot the message: "Start at the beginning and make sure you get the little things right. It is just one of the many lessons I still carry over to this day from those camps."

Helin attended a Wooden camp two summers and said that the experience created "some of the best memories of my childhood."

Years later, when Helin was in college, he took a job at a restaurant and was surprised to learn that it was one of Coach Wooden's favorite eateries. Whenever Coach came for dinner, Helin seated him in a quiet, secluded corner of the restaurant so that no one would bother him during his meal. When Helin came by to refill his iced tea glass, Coach engaged him in conversation, asking about his life, his post-college plans, and his side job as a local sportswriter for the *Los Angeles Daily News*. Those conversations were small gestures on Coach Wooden's part, yet they had a huge impact on young Kurt Helin.

"Like so many people who crossed paths with John Wooden," he concluded, "I went in expecting one thing and came out with lessons that lasted a lifetime. Things that didn't sink in to a fourth-grader but do to a guy still around the game every day in another capacity. To a guy who is a husband. To a guy who is a father. To a guy who wants to be a better person."[1]

Little details are vital to success in life. Little things make big things happen.

A Foundation of Fundamentals

On those Sunday afternoons as camp began, Coach talked about the attitude he expected from campers. Be a good student of the game and of life by being industrious, enthusiastic, dependable, loyal, and cooperative. Work constantly to improve—never become complacent and satisfied with where you are. Basketball is a game of habits, and it takes time and patient effort to build those habits. Work hard and earn the right to be confident. Acquire peace of mind by becoming the best you can be. He also talked about the behavior he expected from campers. Be on time—all the time. Keep your emotions under control, yet never lose your competitive spirit. Work to achieve the best possible physical, mental, and moral conditioning. Never criticize or attack a teammate. Never expect favors. Never waste time. Never make excuses. Never grandstand, never boast, never sulk, never be lazy. Discipline yourself so others don't have to.

> *Never criticize or attack a teammate. Never expect favors. Never waste time. Never make excuses.*

Coach talked about the team spirit he expected from campers. Be a team player. The game of basketball requires that you work together as a team. Learn the fundamentals of the game while practicing the fundamentals of life—how to live together, work together, support one another, and be considerate of one another.

The contribution of any athlete in a team sport, Coach said, is based on three essential factors: (1) physical conditioning, achieved through daily organized practices, supervised by a coach, along with a player's hard work and good conduct between practices; (2) proper execution of the fundamentals, which can be achieved only through hard work and repeated drills in practice; and (3) teamwork, which Coach defined as "an eagerness to sacrifice personal interests or glory for the welfare of the team." Teamwork requires an attitude of consideration toward others and humility about oneself. Great teammates know that giving comes before receiving.

Coach Wooden usually concluded his opening talk with a statement he would make several more times throughout the week:

"My personal definition of success is 'peace of mind, which can be attained only through self-satisfaction in knowing you made the effort to do the best of which you are capable.'"

Dave Burgess—an educator, a speaker, and the bestselling author of *Teach Like a Pirate*—got into teaching as a basketball coach at a high school in San Diego. He told me his approach to teaching was influenced by the time he spent as a counselor at Wooden's camps. "John Wooden often said that coaching is teaching and teaching is coaching," Burgess said. "You can't separate them. He was first and foremost a teacher, and he focused on teaching fundamental skills. I worked for Coach Wooden at the camps for three years, starting when I was about sixteen. Coach told us that to be competitive you don't have to do extraordinary things. You simply have to do ordinary things extraordinarily well. He told us that every detail is important when it comes to being the best you can be.

"Details matter. That's why Coach Wooden focused so intensely on fundamental skills. I learned this while working at his camps. Later, after I became a basketball coach, I'd shake my head at some of the teams we played. They could run fifteen different out-of-bounds plays from underneath the basket, but their kids couldn't jump stop. Those teams had prioritized running a bunch of out-of-bounds plays over fundamental skill development. I learned from Coach Wooden that it really comes down to mastering the fundamentals. To see him drilling the campers in the fundamentals, much as he had drilled his Division I college players, said a lot to me about the importance of the fundamentals."

Coach's attention to detail was so meticulous that he even instructed his players on how to stand up their shoes against the wall at the end of the day. He told them to set their shoes at an angle so that the shoes would air out and any dampness would evaporate. I've heard again and again from Coach Wooden's campers and former players that they still put on their socks and shoes as he instructed them, and they still stand up their shoes at an angle against the wall at night.

One of Coach Wooden's former campers, John Brooks, told me, "Fifteen or more years into our marriage, I was still standing my shoes against the wall to air out, just as Coach Wooden had taught us. I was explaining to my young son the importance of airing out his shoes that way, and I told him I had learned the method from Coach Wooden when I was in his basketball camp. My wife happened to be standing there, listening to this, and she said, 'Oh! For all these years, I've wondered why you set your shoes up against the wall like that. Now I know.'"

Did Coach Wooden's string of championships begin with something as simple as how his players put on socks and shoes? Coach thought so. And so do I. "I've tried to teach my college players how important it is to put on your socks and shoes the right way," Coach told his campers. "Sometimes my players laughed at that. But I didn't care! As long as they learned to pay attention to these details, I didn't care if they thought it was silly. I knew it would help them become better players, and that's all I wanted."

Socks and shoes may be a small detail in the big scheme of things, but as Coach so convincingly demonstrated, little things make big things happen.

Simple, Fundamental Balance

Mike Thibault began his pro basketball career as a scout and assistant coach with the Los Angeles Lakers. He served in similar positions with the Chicago Bulls when the team acquired Michael Jordan, Charles Oakley, and John Paxson. He is currently the coach of the WNBA's Washington Mystics. Thibault told me, "I worked at the Wooden summer basketball camps for five years—three weeks each summer. I was still working at the camps during my first year on the Lakers' staff. I continue to put on basketball clinics to this day, and I teach the principles and fundamentals I learned at Coach Wooden's camps.

"Coach had a profound influence on me. He was a stickler for teaching the fundamentals of basketball. He made all the coaches at his camps pay attention to the fundamentals. He wanted everyone to be alert and quick in their movements on the court. We did a lot of repetition so that good habits became ingrained.

"I can speak for all the coaches at the camps when I say that we all wanted to be like Coach Wooden, even though he stressed to us young coaches again and again, 'Be yourself.' He said, 'You can learn from me and other coaches, but you have to be who you are.' And the best way to really discover our own style as coaches, he said, was by staying focused on the fundamentals."

Fundamentals are those basic basketball skills players must master to effectively play the game. They include dribbling, ball-handling, shooting, doing layups, passing, rebounding, setting screens and picks, and so forth. Coach Wooden always spent most of his teaching time helping his players—and campers—master the fundamentals. But perhaps the simplest and most basic skill Coach taught his campers was how to maintain their balance. Here's a typical talk by Coach Wooden on the importance of maintaining balance in basketball and in life.

"The most important word in the world is *love*. If we all had love for one another, we wouldn't need any other words, because love says it all. The second most important word is *balance*. Balance is so important in basketball and in life. We must have balance. We mustn't get carried away. We mustn't get too low when things go wrong, and we mustn't get too high and overconfident when things go well. We must keep our emotions in balance. We must keep everything in perspective.

"Now, we all need good balance to play the game of basketball. The first thing to understand about maintaining your balance is that your physical balance is controlled by the three extremities of the body. What are those three extremities? The first extremity is the feet. And what's the extremity farthest away from the feet? The head. And what is the third extremity? The hands.

"To play the game properly and maintain your balance, you have to keep your

"Balance is so important in basketball and in life."

feet slightly wider apart than your shoulders. You have to keep your head directly above the midpoint between your feet. If you lean too far forward, too far backward, or too far to either side, you'll lose your balance. Your head is made of bone and water, so it's a heavy substance, isn't it? You have to keep your head up. You'd better keep your chin up. If you tuck your chin down against your chest, you can't see anything. You must keep your head up so you can see.

"Next, you must keep your hands in close to maintain your balance. When you have a basketball in your hands, keep it close to the body, not extended away from the body. In here, close to your chest, not way out there. When shooting, shoot from close in here, from the center of the body. Keep your elbows directly above your knees. Keep your knee directly above the foot. Keep your hand directly above the elbow. Keep your head directly above the midpoint between the feet, and the feet just wider than the shoulders. Keep them all in line as you go up and shoot. That's how you maintain balance while shooting.

"Balance is equally important in rebounding. When you get the ball, bring it in close to the body. If you keep it out here, away from the body, someone will take it. So in basketball, the extremities of the body determine your physical balance.

"So you have the three extremities of the body—the head, the hands, and the feet. Between these extremities you have joints—knees, hips, elbows, shoulders. Don't be caught with your knees and elbows straight and rigid. Keep them relaxed all the time. If you get tight and tense, if you extend those joints, you won't have balance, you won't have freedom of movement, and you won't play a good game of basketball. Keep your knees and elbows flexed. When you pass, receive, shoot, or rebound, keep the ball close to the body to maintain your balance and protect the ball from your opponents. If you remember those simple principles, you'll become a better basketball player.

"But you can't have physical balance without *mental* balance, because the message that comes from the brain tells the feet and the hands what to do. You also can't have physical balance without *emotional* balance. You can't play well if you are angry and out of control. So you must keep your mind and your emotions balanced and under control all the time."

A Basketball Skill—and a Metaphor for Life

As a master communicator, Coach Wooden understood the importance of making ideas visible and memorable with the use of visual aids. On one occasion, while talking about the importance of balance as a fundamental basketball skill, he spotted a twelve-year-old girl sitting on the gym floor with a book balanced on her head. "I see a young lady out there," he said, "who is probably planning to become a model. She is practicing the skill of holding her head up high with a book balanced on it. When you play basketball, you have to maintain that kind of commitment and intention to maintaining your balance."

Coach later learned that the young lady in question was not planning a modeling career after all. She was a fan and admirer who had brought a book to be autographed. The book she had balanced on her head was Coach Wooden's 1972 autobiography, *They Call Me Coach*. But no matter—she had helped Coach make his point about balance in a visual and memorable way.

During the morning workouts, Coach drilled his campers in the fundamental skill of maintaining their balance at all times in all circumstances. He drilled them on footwork, technique, and visualization, showing them how to shoot an imaginary ball at an imaginary basket while maintaining their balance. He showed them how to keep the imaginary ball close to the chest, arms close to the body, stance wide, head over the midpoint of the stance. With practice and repetition, the campers were soon performing these drills with flawless precision.

Throughout each drill, even when he was in his eighties, Coach shouted out instructions and encouragement with the energy and authority of a much younger coach. Just as his UCLA players had done in their practices, Coach's campers clapped their hands in rhythm during the drills to keep up a brisk tempo. This rhythm also motivated the campers to practice hard in spite of fatigue.

Camp counselor Howard Fisher recalled the impact of these drills on his life when he was a camper at age thirteen. "These repetitive fundamental drills," he said, "had a big impact on me when I was a player. For two weeks after camp ended, I continued to do these simple fundamental drills on my own in my grandparents' driveway."[2]

Coach not only taught balance as an essential skill for the game of basketball but also used balance in basketball to teach the importance of physical, mental, emotional, and moral balance in life. Coach Wooden was so much more than a basketball coach. To borrow what has become a somewhat overused term, Coach Wooden was truly a *life coach*. To everyone who encountered him—his players, his campers, his counselors, his coaches, and me as well—he was truly a man who coached in the game of life.

There Are No Trivial Details

Over a forty-year coaching career, Coach Wooden compiled a record of 885 wins, 203 losses, and 10 national championships—and he attributed his success as a coach to a lot of little things done well. He once wrote:

> High performance and production are achieved only through the identification and perfection of small but relevant details—little things done well. . . . I derived great satisfaction from identifying and perfecting those "trivial" and often troublesome details, because I knew, without doubt, that each one brought UCLA a bit closer to our goal: competitive greatness. If you collect enough pennies you'll eventually be rich. Each relevant and perfect detail was another penny in our bank.[3]

On another occasion, he wrote, "In my profession, fundamentals included such 'trivial' issues as insisting on double-tying of shoelaces, seeing that uniforms were properly fitted, and getting players in position to rebound every missed shot. The perfection of those little things—making a habit of doing them right—usually determines if a job is done well or done poorly."[4]

When we focus on the fundamentals, we can break down big, intimidating problems into smaller, solvable challenges. When our problems become manageable and solvable, our fear evaporates and our confidence soars. This approach to teaching is called the "whole-part" approach because it breaks down the whole into fundamental parts. *Sports Illustrated*'s Alexander Wolff observed that Coach Wooden taught by breaking down every concept into its fundamentals:

> Wooden taught by using the "whole-part" method, breaking the game down to its elements—"just like parsing a sentence," he would say, sounding like the English teacher he had indeed once been. He applied the four basic laws of learning: explanation, demonstration, correction, and repetition. And he developed a pedagogy resting on the notion that basketball is a game of threes: forward, center, guard; shoot, drive, pass; ball, you, man; conditioning, skill, teamwork.

As a coach who shunned recruiting, put relatively little stock in the scouting of opponents, and refused to equate success with winning, Wooden figured to have become a great failure rather than college sports' preeminent winner of all time. An article of faith among coaches holds that one must be intolerant of mistakes, but here, too, Wooden was a contrarian. He considered errors to be precious opportunities for teaching—preferably in practice, of course. And the games were exams.[5]

Retired basketball coach Myron Finkbeiner told me about a time he watched Coach Wooden putting his UCLA Bruins through practice drills in preparation for the 1975 Final Four. "It was amazing to watch them," he said, "because Coach put them through the same drills he had used on the first day of practice at the beginning of the season. They ran through simple little passing drills, pivoting moves, blocking out routines. John Wooden was redoing the fundamentals all over again." And those were precisely the same drills he put his campers through at his basketball camps.

His single-minded focus on the fundamentals went back to his days as a teacher and coach at South Bend Central High School in Indiana. In South Bend, Coach befriended Notre Dame football coach Frank Leahy, who invited him to visit a Notre Dame football practice. Coach Wooden observed how Leahy's players moved rapidly from drill to drill at the sound of his whistle. Practices were not long, but they were well-organized and fast-paced—and amazingly effective. Years later, Coach observed:

> Organization became a primary asset of my coaching methodology—the ability to use time with great efficiency. . . . There wasn't one second in the whole practice when anybody was standing around wondering what would come next. . . . The whole thing was synchronized; each hour offered up sixty minutes, and I squeezed every second out of every minute.
>
> Players felt, at times, that the actual game against an opponent was slower than our practice in the gym. That's exactly the way I designed it.[6]

The point of drilling the fundamentals was to transform a learned skill into an instinctive habit. Coach once told an interviewer, "Our UCLA teams . . . kept it simple. Our opponents always said we were easy to scout but difficult to play because we executed well."[7]

The secret of Coach Wooden's success was that he enabled his players and his campers to execute the fundamentals automatically and without an eyeblink of hesitation. To be successful in any aspect of life, follow the formula Coach Wooden demonstrated: Focus on the fundamentals. Practice balance. Break your goal into smaller parts. Then repeat.

The Secret of Success

André McCarter played basketball at UCLA from 1973 to 1976—and for a long time, he battled Coach Wooden's hardheaded insistence on the fundamentals. Once when McCarter made one of his showboat behind-the-back passes to a teammate, Coach Wooden uttered his strongest oath: "Goodness gracious sakes alive, André!"

Now, that may not sound like an angry outburst, but Coach Wooden's players knew that when he said, "Goodness gracious sakes alive!" it was time to be afraid. Coach never swore, but he did get angry—and those mild-sounding words could strike fear in the heart of a Bruin. Coach was a firm disciplinarian, and he insisted that his players play the game *his* way. Though some of his players loved to wow the crowds with razzle-dazzle moves, Coach viewed show-off passes as risky gambles that led to costly turnovers.

So Coach called McCarter on the carpet and reminded him, "We use the basic chest pass here at UCLA." That reprimand rubbed McCarter the wrong way. He and Coach Wooden continued to butt heads over the next few weeks until Coach finally took McCarter out of the starting lineup. Somehow, McCarter survived his first season as a Bruin, but on the first day of practice his sophomore year, McCarter again incurred the wrath of Wooden.

During a practice game, McCarter stole an inbounded ball from the opponent and sprinted downcourt. Coach had taught his players to pass to a wide-open teammate for an easy score. But McCarter faked a behind-the-back pass, kept the ball, and made the bucket himself. His wide-open teammate, star center Bill Walton, watched open-jawed and flat-footed.

McCarter's stunt was a total negation of Coach Wooden's focus-on-the-fundamentals approach to the game. "Goodness gracious sakes alive, André!" a livid Coach Wooden shouted. "You do that again and you won't play on our team!"

Frustrated and angry, McCarter seriously considered leaving UCLA, but his mother talked him out of quitting. "Coach Wooden won a bunch of championships before you got there," she said. "He must know something you haven't figured out yet."

McCarter, who was raised in a Bible-believing home, decided to pray about the conflict between himself and Coach Wooden. "Lord," he said, "give me the strength to put my ego aside. Help me change my attitude."

After he prayed, he felt God prompting him to learn everything he could about Coach Wooden. So he went to the library and looked up magazine articles about Coach Wooden—his life, his beliefs, and his basketball philosophy. He also studied Coach Wooden's Pyramid of Success.

A few days later, Coach gave a talk to the team, saying, "Winning basketball has nothing to do with the highlight plays you see on TV. Teams win because they play unselfishly, and their players have solid fundamentals." For the first time since becoming a Bruin, McCarter understood what Coach was saying to him—and he realized that Coach had a deeper purpose in mind than winning basketball games. He was trying to *change lives*. "Basketball,"

McCarter later said, "was just something to prepare us to be good students of life."

From that day forward, McCarter became a student of the fundamentals. The change in his attitude was so profound that Coach later made him starting point guard and encouraged him to be a leader on the team. After UCLA's victory over Kentucky in the 1975 national championship game—Coach Wooden's tenth and final championship—Coach hugged McCarter and told him, "You were my coach on the floor."

That compliment left McCarter choked up and emotional. He had learned a lesson that would serve him well throughout his life. He was glad that Coach had finally gotten this message through to him: it's the little things, the fundamentals, that make you a consistent winner.[8]

Decades later, after Coach Wooden passed away, McCarter wrote a remembrance of Coach that was posted on the Christian Broadcasting Network's website. "Coach Wooden always enforced the little details and it led to championships," he wrote. "Coach taught us how to put on our socks; no wrinkles in the socks meant no blisters on the feet. The practical application of wrinkle free socks is the equivalent to Song of Solomon 2:15. The Word says to identify and deconstruct the little foxes that will spoil the vine. This is a powerful principle in maintaining a healthy marriage, business relationships, and sports teams."[9]

> *"The closest I have ever come to one secret of success is this: a lot of little things done well."*

In basketball and in life, the little details are vital. I learned this principle from Coach Wooden himself. During one of our dinners together, I asked him, "Coach, if you could pinpoint just one secret of success in life, what would it be?" Then I leaned in closer, not wanting to miss a single syllable of his wisdom.

"Pat," he said, "the closest I have ever come to one secret of success is this: a lot of little things done well."

That's what he succeeded in teaching a young point guard named André McCarter. That's what he tried to instill in all his UCLA teams. And that's what he continued to teach, summer after summer, to the hundreds of campers in his basketball camps. Focus on the fundamentals. Do all the little things well. Repeat and repeat until fundamental skills become unconscious habits. Execute the little things flawlessly.

Then watch what happens!

3

Be a Leader
Who Builds Leaders

A leader's most powerful ally is his or her own
example.

Coach John Wooden

My friend Keith Glass is CEO of Glass Global Sports Group and
the author of the sports memoir *Taking Shots* (2007). Over a
three-decade-long career, he has negotiated contracts for more
than two hundred athletes in the United States, Europe, and Asia.
He's a very successful sports agent.

But when Glass was twenty-seven years old, attending law school
in Southern California, he was struggling to make ends meet. When
he needed a summer job, he asked college coach Larry Brown
for suggestions. Brown said, "Go to John Wooden and ask for a
coaching job in his basketball camps."

Glass applied for a job and was hired as a coach. He would earn
$150 a week for the three weeks. That doesn't sound like much

money today, but Glass was thrilled to have a job teaching kids how to play basketball.

When Glass arrived at the camp, he noticed a young man who shadowed Coach Wooden all day long. Whenever Coach needed anything, he'd tell this young man, and off he'd go. Keith asked one of the camp directors, "Who is that guy? What does he do?"

"Oh, he's the commissioner of the camps. He's with Coach all day long and does anything Coach needs him to do."

Glass said, "That's the job I want! What does it pay?"

"Seventy-five dollars a week—half of what you make as a coach."

"I want that job," Glass said, "even at half pay."

And sure enough, he got the job.

"I had no money," Glass told me, "but I gladly took the pay cut for the chance to spend all day with John Wooden. You couldn't put a price tag on that."

Part of Glass's job involved driving Coach Wooden. (The camp directors later devised a system in which counselors drove Coach on a rotating basis.) So in the summer of 1975, Glass was Coach Wooden's chauffeur and assistant.

"Coach was a regular, humble guy," Glass told me. "He'd just won his tenth NCAA title in twelve years, and I was driving him in my beat-up four-cylinder car. The camp was in the mountains, and there were times I wondered whether my old puddle jumper would get up over the mountains. It was hot, and I had no air-conditioning, but Coach never complained.

"Next to my father, Coach Wooden was the best man I've ever met. I would pick him up at six, and we'd get out to the college gym for the day's work. We'd be the first ones there. He wanted to be there early to check the facility and make sure everything was in place.

"He'd go around to all the drinking fountains with paper towels, and he'd clean the drinking fountains himself. The campers would spit out their gum in the drinking fountains, so there'd be pieces of gum in the bowls. It was kind of disgusting, but Coach would make sure the drinking fountains were shiny and clean.

"The example Coach set by doing things like that made a big impression on me. Coach didn't preach. He lived his lessons. He set an example. Whenever you were around him, it was lesson after lesson. He'd never say, 'This is how you should lead,' but if you had eyes to see and ears to hear, you'd learn by watching the man.

"Throughout the camp, I'd take Coach from his condo to Cal Lutheran and back. Some days when I'd pick him up at six in the morning, I hadn't even been to bed yet. I'd come to his condo, and Coach would say, 'Good morning, young man!' And he knew I'd been out all night, but he didn't give me a hard time about it.

"The last day I drove him he said, 'Keith, would you like to come into my condo?' I said, 'Yes, of course.' Coach said, 'One condition, Keith. You're not to tell other people about what I have in here.' He meant his awards and trophies and so forth—he didn't ever want a spotlight shone on his accomplishments. So I agreed, and we went inside.

"Coach went into a back room and returned with a box. He took out a copy of his Pyramid of Success and handed it to me. 'Would you like to have this?' I said, 'Wow, Coach, I'd love to have that.' He said, 'Would you like it signed?' Well, of course I wanted it signed. Who wouldn't? But Coach was so humble that he didn't assume anything. I said, 'I'd be very happy if you'd sign it.' And he did. And I was.

"I didn't realize it at the time," Glass concluded, "but those camps were not just about teaching basketball to campers. Coach was teaching his coaches how to teach. He was teaching the teachers and leading the leaders."

Just Three Secrets

Mike Kunstadt coached basketball at a high school in Corpus Christi, Texas, and later became a coach with the John Wooden Basketball

Fundamentals Camp. How did he become acquainted with Coach Wooden? Well, he simply picked up the phone and called.

Kunstadt's high school team had made the play-offs for the first time. "I was nervous about it," he explained, "so out of the blue I decided to call Coach Wooden and ask for advice. He was still the coach at UCLA at the time." Kunstadt had never met Coach, never corresponded with him, and had to call directory assistance to get his number at UCLA.

"I called expecting to get his secretary," he said, "but Coach answered. . . . He told me about his Pyramid, which I had never heard of before. He said, 'Fully prepare your team, make sure the players prepare themselves, and hopefully the outcome will be favorable. But if not, have peace that you did your best, that you did all you could.'"

Coach Wooden gave Kunstadt permission to record the call. Kunstadt played the recording for his players, and they were so inspired by Coach Wooden's message that they battled all the way to the high school Final Four. After the season ended, Kunstadt wrote Coach Wooden, telling him how much his message had inspired the team from Corpus Christi. Then Kunstadt asked Coach if he could work at Wooden's basketball camps.

Coach made the arrangements, and that summer Mike Kunstadt coached all three weeks. His wife, Gerri, became good friends with Coach's wife, Nell, and a few years later, Coach Wooden stayed with Coach Kunstadt's family when he went to Texas to receive the Theodore Roosevelt Award.

Coach Wooden was always generous with his time, his wisdom, and his advice. He was eager to open doors for other coaches and to help them become stronger, more capable leaders. He truly was a coach of coaches and a leader of leaders.

Retired basketball coach Dale Brown led the Louisiana State University Tigers for twenty-five years, coaching the Tigers to Final Four appearances in 1981 and 1986. Nicknamed the "Master Motivator," Brown was an inspirational leader who demonstrated a Wooden-like ability to get the best performances out of modestly talented teams. Soon after he was hired by LSU in 1972, Brown called Coach Wooden for advice (by that time, Coach had won eight of his eventual ten national championships).

Coach Wooden invited Brown to visit him for a few days at his home in Encino. So Brown arrived at Coach Wooden's home at eight o'clock one morning, planning to take a few hours of Coach's day, then return the following day. They talked and talked, and Brown realized it was nearly six in the evening. He had monopolized Coach Wooden's entire day.

"Coach," he said, "I've taken enough of your time. I'm sure you're tired. I'll come back tomorrow."

"No, Dale," Coach said. "I'm not tired. We'll continue." They talked until 10:30 that night.

Over the next few days, Coach gave Brown an intensive course in the art of coaching. Brown, meanwhile, filled a thick notebook with wisdom from Coach Wooden.

On their last day together, Coach said, "You could have saved a lot of time taking so many notes. There are really just three secrets to effective coaching."

Brown leaned closer, ready to receive the wisdom of the ages.

"The three things that I am going to tell you are fairly simple," Coach said. "First, make certain that you always have better players than anybody that you play. Make sure you always get those better players to put the team above themselves; that is imperative. Finally, don't try to be some coaching genius or guru. Don't give your players

"Always practice simplicity with constant repetition."

too much information. Remember there are only five variables or players on the court. Always practice simplicity with constant repetition."

Over his next quarter century as a coach, Brown returned again and again to Coach Wooden's three secrets. "From the first time that

I met him," he later reflected, "I knew he would be my life's most significant mentor. . . . He was a teacher, always ready to help."[1]

I asked Brown the most important lesson he learned from Coach Wooden. "He was my mentor for forty years," Brown told me, "so he taught me many unforgettable lessons. But maybe the most important of all is this: Talent is God-given, so be humble. Fame is man-given, so be thankful. Conceit is self-given, so be careful.

"In a long conversation at his home one night, Coach told me, 'There is no area of basketball in which I am a genius. None. Tactically and strategically, I'm just average—and this is not false modesty. We won national championships while I was coaching at UCLA because I was above average in analyzing players, getting them to fill roles as part of a team, and we practiced simplicity with constant repetition, day after day, with great players.' My dear friend Coach Wooden was an American treasure. As a teacher and a mentor, he was absolutely selfless and generous with his time and his wisdom."

Mike Kunstadt summed up the essence of Coach Wooden: "Coach is so famous and successful, but he makes time for people."[2] Coach Wooden was a leader who continually inspired and encouraged other leaders. He was a coach of coaches.

Coaching the Wooden Way

Every morning after breakfast, Coach Wooden's first order of camp business was leadership training. He met with his coaches and showed them how to teach basketball the Coach Wooden way. He reminded his coaches of three essential concepts they needed to get across:

1. The campers needed to get in the best possible physical and mental condition.
2. The campers needed to learn not only the fundamentals of basketball but also how to execute those fundamentals quickly.

3. The campers needed to learn to play together as a team.

While Coach insisted that his coaches instruct the campers in the UCLA high post offense, he stressed that no one offense or defense could bring the most out of the players. "Your job is to get the most out of what you have," Coach told them. "The more you worry about what the other teams have, the less you are going to do with what you have."[3]

Greg Hayes spoke for many coaches who worked at the camps: "The Sportsworld brochure advertising the John Wooden camps reads, 'Learn to play better basketball the Coach Wooden way.' Those of us who are coaches, however, want to learn to *coach* better basketball the Coach Wooden way."[4]

Ask anyone who coached at a Wooden camp what he remembers most fondly, and you'll probably hear, "Mealtimes with Coach." Retired basketball coach Jim Harrick, who coached at UCLA, Pepperdine, Rhode Island, and Georgia, was Coach Wooden's first camp director in 1971. He recalled that sharing a meal with Coach Wooden was like "getting a doctorate degree in basketball." Sometimes Coach's food would grow cold as he talked game strategy with his coaches, shifting water glasses and salt and pepper shakers around on the table to simulate

> *"The more you worry about what the other teams have, the less you are going to do with what you have."*

players. At other times, Coach would wax philosophical about such issues as love, respect, and competition. Harrick often had to blow his whistle to end those mealtime sessions.[5]

Longtime baseball executive Bill Bavasi worked as a counselor at the Wooden basketball camps during the summer between his freshman and sophomore years at the University of San Diego. "They paid me twenty-five dollars a week to be a camp counselor," Bavasi told me. "Later, they made me head counselor and raised my pay to fifty dollars a week. There were two of us counselors who took turns picking Coach up and driving him home. So I got to spend time talking with Coach every other day.

"He didn't seem to mind riding with me in my little Volkswagen Rabbit. He was engaging and always interested in my questions and in what I had to say. He was always teaching and mentoring. I could tell he really enjoyed teaching young people who were willing to listen—and that was certainly me. I respected him for what he had achieved as a coach, but even more important, I liked him as a human being and a teacher. Those times when I drove him to camp and back in my little VW were some of the most life-changing moments of my life."

A Leader Who Listened

Before the Sunday afternoon meeting with coaches and parents, Coach Wooden conducted a meeting with his camp coaches. Fortunately, Greg Hayes had the foresight to take a video camera into one of Coach Wooden's meetings with his coaches so that the leadership wisdom Coach shared would be preserved. Coach started by making sure his coaches had realistic expectations for the campers. "Our goal," he said, "is not to make the campers into stars. . . . Those lacking God-given skills can never attain so-called star status in our camp. But we can help them bring about improvement at every level if they are attentive and industrious."

He made clear that his coaches would be teaching campers to execute the fundamentals: "Emphasize quickness and balance in the execution of all fundamentals. Both are very important. But accuracy must not be sacrificed for quickness. Teach balance in all things—basketball and life. . . . In all things show consideration of others."

Next, Coach Wooden reminded his coaches of their solemn responsibility as leaders and educators: "Remember that you are a teacher, and you must teach. Be positive and show great patience, and do not expect too much too soon. Don't neglect the less gifted for the more gifted."

Coach stressed that his coaches needed to show fairness on the court: "All players should get to play in at least half of the game and must participate in each half, even in the championship games, regardless of their ability. Emphasize doing their best rather than the score. . . . Stress team balance—equal opportunities for all."

Above all, Coach Wooden expected his coaches to be role models of good sportsmanship and considerate behavior: "There will be no talking to or criticizing officials. . . . Use no profanity, and permit none. This is very important. Do not allow campers to goof off. Be on guard about hurting the feelings of any player. Be careful and constructive in your criticism, and refrain from the use of sarcasm. Remember to be positive."

Finally, Coach reminded his coaches why they were there: to impact the campers' lives. "The success of this camp will depend largely upon your efforts and cooperation. Together I hope we can make this a truly rewarding experience for every camper."[6]

You may not always like what your players do, Coach Wooden told his coaches, but you must always love them. A good teacher corrects his students without provoking them to anger. A teacher can't antagonize his students and expect to achieve positive results. Don't use sarcasm. Don't embarrass a player. Command respect—not by throwing your authority around but by earning it through the way you lead your players.

As a leader, Coach Wooden was a great example of the balance between being a good listener and being a firm decision maker. "I never knew Coach to be close-minded," Craig Impelman told me. "He invited ideas and critiques from the staff. After every camp, he would conduct a wrap-up session in which the leaders talked about what worked and what didn't. Everyone got to offer suggestions. After Coach listened to everyone's ideas, he would make the decision. But he always listened with an open mind."

Impelman showed me a three-page handwritten memo from one of the camp directors with suggestions for improving the camp. In the right margin, written in Coach Wooden's distinctive black Sharpie handwriting, were Coach's preliminary reactions. Most of Coach's responses were a single positive word, such as "Good" or "Agree" or "Yes" or "Okay." Coach didn't respond to any suggestion with a negative, though he did greet some suggestions with the word "Discuss" or even a question mark.

Former LSU head basketball coach Dale Brown told me about conversations he had with two of Coach Wooden's top assistants at UCLA. Brown said, "Jerry Norman told me that one of the clues to Coach Wooden's success was his willingness to listen to others. Jerry said, 'John Wooden was a very smart person, and he knew what he did not know. He was a very attentive listener to new ideas.' And another outstanding UCLA assistant coach, Denny Crum, told me, 'Coach would only make a change if you strongly convinced him with all the facts why it would work. You had to prove it to him, you had to debate him—but he listened, and once you convinced him, he would change.'"

Because Coach was an open-minded listener, his camps continually improved summer after summer. He understood that the best ideas often come from those on the front lines. He was a leader who taught—and a leader who listened.

A Coach of Coaches

Ronn Wyckoff is a cofounder of the National Basketball Shooters Association, an organization that encourages athletes to develop their skills in free throw shooting. In 1974, Wyckoff coached at the John Wooden Basketball Fundamentals Camp during a summer break from his job as a high school basketball coach. He brought his son Sean, and while Wyckoff was working with high-school-age campers, Sean participated in the nine-and-ten-year-old group. One day Wyckoff took Coach aside for a private chat.

"I explained to him," Wyckoff recalled, "that since I hadn't played in college, I didn't see my chances as very good to go beyond coaching high school."

Coach Wooden listened carefully, then offered a suggestion that changed Wyckoff's life. He suggested that Wyckoff consider international coaching. Wyckoff had never thought of going outside the United States. He thanked Coach and soon began researching opportunities overseas. Working with the People-To-People Sports Committee, he took a position coaching the national basketball program for the African nation of Rhodesia (now Zimbabwe). The following year he worked with programs in several Caribbean countries and later in Sweden and Norway.

Those experiences gave him the credentials to become a sought-after speaker at coaching clinics in the United States and elsewhere. His new speaking career led to a book and a four-hour DVD program called *Basketball on a Triangle: A Higher Level of Coaching and Playing*. And it all began with a brief conversation with Coach Wooden.

Once in 1973, Ronn Wyckoff took his school's varsity boys basketball team to witness a UCLA practice. Wyckoff, his seven-year-old son, and his players sat in the bleachers in Pauley Pavilion watching the players doing warm-ups on the floor.

Coach Wooden came over to introduce himself. He told Wyckoff's players, "Listen to your coach and do everything he tells you. If you do that, you'll be winners."

And Wyckoff's team did win that season. "We beat bigger teams than ourselves," he recalled. "We won our league and we ended up in the Southern California play-offs for small schools. My players came back from the UCLA visit excited and fired up."[7]

Coach Wooden was a leader of leaders, a teacher of teachers, and a coach of coaches.

A Mentor of Mentors

Cori Close has been the head women's basketball coach for the UCLA Bruins since 2011. Her Bruins completed the 2015–16 season with a 26-9 overall record and a 14-4 Pac-10 Conference record. In 1994, when she was an assistant coach at UCLA, one of the men's assistants, Steve Lavin, said to her, "Let's go see Coach Wooden." Though the thought of visiting the UCLA legend was intimidating, she agreed to go.

When Lavin and Close arrived at his Encino condo, Coach Wooden immediately put Close at ease. "From that point on," she recalled, "I pretty much went back every other Tuesday for the rest of my time as an assistant at UCLA, and then I continued to come back once a month, even after I went to coach at the University of Santa Barbara. That went on for nine straight years."[8] Throughout that time, Close was personally mentored by Coach Wooden—and it shows in the way she coaches at UCLA.

"Coach Wooden was a great mentor," she said, "because he lived what he taught. He was a brilliant teacher. He knew how to communicate in a way that just really hit your heart, and then he just really loved you unconditionally."

Mentoring, Close said, is about investing in the lives of other people, expecting nothing in return. As a result of watching Coach's example, she said, "I don't care about my own legacy, to be honest. Coach Wooden didn't care about his either. That's what made it so powerful. The legacy he wanted was just to pour [his influence] into people. He wanted his legacy to be that he treated *all* people really well. And then hopefully they would treat other people really well."

Close saw that Coach treated everyone the same, from the rich and famous to the janitorial staff. He took an interest in everybody, he talked to everybody, he showed kindness to everybody. She attributes Coach Wooden's exemplary life to his deep faith. "I think a big part of Coach Wooden's ability to stay grounded was his faith," she said. "He would say, 'Drink deeply from good books, first and foremost, the Bible.' I think he spent a lot of time there, and his faith was a grounding point."[9]

Phil Grant is a retired high school basketball coach who formerly taught at Brawley High in the Imperial Valley of California. He still conducts basketball camps and clinics for young people. Grant used to coach at Coach Wooden's basketball camps, and his favorite memories of the camps involved driving Coach to and from the camps, all the while being mentored by Coach Wooden himself.

"Coach was always mentoring," Grant told me. "He didn't so much mentor the campers, but he was always mentoring the coaches and counselors at the camps. He would share his knowledge and embrace them and empower them. Then the coaches and counselors would go to their teams and dorm rooms and have a mentoring impact in the lives of the campers.

"No matter how busy he was or how tired he might be, Coach was always generous with his time, always willing to stop and talk and give of himself. He didn't just show up for an hour to give a talk, then disappear. He'd be at the camp all day.

"Coach was consistent; he was a rock. His values were built on the rock-solid values of old-time America, and that attracted all of us to him. Years later, some of us would see him at an event—and he remembered *everybody*. By *name*. He never forgot you, in spite of all the people he met over the years. He was more than a teacher, more than a coach. Once you met him, once you worked with him, he was your mentor and your friend for life."

Steve Hawkins, head basketball coach at Western Michigan University in Kalamazoo, was also mentored by Coach Wooden.

He coached at the camps and was one of Coach's many camp chauffeurs. He recalled one time when he was driving and Coach said, "Steve, pick up Tom on the next block." Steve didn't know who Tom was, but he pulled up at the corner—and there stood Tom Landry, head coach of the Dallas Cowboys.

So there was young Steve Hawkins driving his van with two of the most famous coaches in the world as his passengers. He said, "All I kept thinking was, I can't crash. I can't be the guy who was responsible for crashing the car with these two coaches."[10]

A Coach's First Priority

One principle Coach Wooden emphasized was that every coach needed to be focused on teaching, not winning. Coaches are, by nature, competitive human beings. They want to win, and there's nothing wrong with that. But Coach Wooden wanted to make sure that the natural competitiveness of his coaches didn't interfere with their first priority: teaching.

Coach made sure his coaches understood that they should not ignore the less-talented players in order to focus on the more-talented players. As Craig Impelman told me, "This was the real hallmark of John Wooden's teaching. He cared about each camper in his camps, and he wanted his coaches to help every camper reach his or her full potential. He didn't cater to the most-skilled players at the camps, and he insisted that his coaches not cater to them either."

In a handout for coaches, Coach Wooden laid out the substitution rules for the teams. It stated, "Please note—every boy must start one game, and if you follow the substitution rules daily, this will occur." Another handout urged coaches to make sure that no camper was neglected or cheated of coaching time: "Help each camper improve in some way, each session."

It's tempting for teachers to cater to the most-gifted students, whether in a classroom or on a basketball court. Coach Wooden believed it was vitally important to resist that temptation and to focus attention on those who needed help the most. He made sure his coaches took time with each camper.

Teaching the Art of Friendship

One of the most frequently asked questions of Coach Wooden was this: Among all the players you coached at UCLA, who were your favorites? "A coach must not have favorites," he replied. "You must not favor one player over another. That doesn't mean you're going to like them all the same. The great college football and basketball coach Alonzo Stagg said, 'I never had a player I didn't love.' But he also said, 'I had a lot I didn't like.'

"A coach must not have favorites."

"Alonzo Stagg understood that you can love somebody without liking him. You can even love people you don't respect. But you must not have favorites. You must not treat players differently because you like one more than you like the other. You don't always treat them exactly the same, but if you treat them differently, it must not be because one is your favorite and the other is not."

After Coach said that, a girl camper stood and asked, "When you say 'love,' do you mean family love or boyfriend love or friend love?"

"Friend love," Coach replied. "We're all family, so in a sense, you have family love on a basketball team as well. But the love we're talking about is friend love. It's not boyfriend-girlfriend love—that's a natural thing we all experience, and there's nothing wrong with that. But the love I'm talking about involves consideration for others, kindness and generosity toward others, apologizing and forgiving one another, accepting other people who are different from you, and accepting people of another race or religion or way of thinking. All of this is rolled up into the kind of love I'm talking about."

At one of Craig Impelman's camps, Coach Wooden explained how friend love should be lived out at camp—and beyond. "My father taught me to make friendship a fine art. Here at camp, I hope you'll make some new friends. Don't just buddy-buddy with the same people you came with all the time. You're going to see them anyway. Don't forget them. Don't cast them aside. Goodness gracious, no. But be sure to take time to make new friends."

Impelman told me how, as the director of his own basketball camps, he learned this lesson from Coach Wooden. "I was running my camps," he said, "and I got a lot of calls from the parents after the first night. They'd say, 'You know, my son is best friends with Billy Jones, who is also at your camp. But my son and Billy aren't on the same team. Could you switch one of them so they're together?' And I'd try to make an accommodation.

"The next year I put it on the camp registration form, a little line where people could indicate a roommate/teammate preference. We tried to accommodate those requests.

"On the first day of the camp, Coach Wooden was talking to the campers. He said, 'Make new friends. Don't just sit and eat lunch with the people you already know. Make an effort to make new friends.' Which, of course, is the opposite of what I had put on the registration form.

"From then on, we left that preference line off the form, and whenever parents called with such a request, we urged parents to persuade their kids to make new friends. I also initiated a policy at all my basketball camps that at lunchtime an older camper had to stand next to a younger camper he didn't know, and the two of them would have lunch together. We made an effort to promote the kind of friendship Coach Wooden talked about."

A Role Model of Organization and Inspiration

"I was continually amazed," Craig Impelman told me, "by the thoroughness of Coach's preparation for the basketball camps. He drew up detailed handouts to prepare the coaches for the practice drills. The handouts described the drills to be run at each station, with the name of the drill, a diagram of the drill, the plays he wanted taught in the drill, and a description of exactly how he wanted it taught.

"What a role model he was! By seeing how thoroughly he prepared us all, I learned how to become a better prepared coach myself. I absorbed lesson after lesson in how to be a better coach. His impact goes far beyond the coaching arena. I consciously try to follow the example he set in the way he lived his life.

"Coach often said, 'You can't live a perfect day without doing something for someone who will never be able to repay you.' Again and again, I saw him live out those words. So I make an effort to do at least one kind thing for someone else, something they can never repay. I might be in the checkout line at the supermarket and notice that the checker has an interesting name, so I smile and say, 'Hey, that's a cool name! You should thank your parents for that name.' Or I might let two or three people go ahead of me in the checkout line. Or I might give a few dollars to a homeless person and say, 'Good luck and God bless you—keep a smile on your face.' That's John Wooden's influence on my life."

> *"You can't live a perfect day without doing something for someone who will never be able to repay you."*

Greg Hayes told me, "Coach Wooden was a leader of leaders. The ripple effect of his influence continues today. His coaches—and I'm one of them—have gone on to spread his influence because of the things he taught us, because of the doors he opened for us, because of the way he inspired and motivated us.

"Many of the coaches from the camps went on to become high school teachers. We became better classroom teachers because of the way Coach taught us. As coaches, we were bonded by our love and respect for Coach Wooden. Most of us returned summer after summer. Many have gone on to run their own basketball camps, spreading Coach Wooden's influence around the world."

I asked Hayes what most impressed him about the way John Wooden mentored his coaches. "It was the way he made us feel important," he said. "Coach spent time with the coaches, and he enjoyed sitting and talking with us. Most of us were high school teachers, and deep down, Coach was still very much a high school teacher himself. He enjoyed being a teacher to the teachers. It felt like he was one of us, and he identified with us. It showed what a caring person Coach was and what a humble nature he had that he enjoyed being around his coaches so much.

"There were many great people coaching at his camps. Coach attracted people who wanted to be there for the right reasons. So Coach Wooden always had a lot in common with his coaches, and I think that's why he enjoyed being with us—and I know that's why we enjoyed being around him."

Coach Never Forgot

Scott Garson is the men's basketball coach at the College of Idaho. He attended a Wooden basketball camp for three summers when he was ten, eleven, and twelve. "I went to the Wooden camps," he told me, "and I got grounded in the fundamentals of basketball. Coach Wooden led all the instruction from up on the stage with his microphone and whistle. He talked about balance, footwork, staying down low, the various pivots, defensive sliding, the fundamentals of shooting. It was the best instruction in the fundamentals of basketball I've ever seen."

I asked Garson what he thought of the coaches at the camps. "It was clear that the coaches had been well instructed in how to teach basketball the Wooden way. Those coaches were not just overseeing a bunch of pickup games—they were teaching the fundamentals. And the teaching was consistent from coach to coach. We rotated between several instructional stations each day, and there were real coaches giving us excellent instruction at each station."

What were Garson's most vivid memories of the camps? "One year," he said, "I got the camper of the year award for my group. It had Coach Wooden's Pyramid of Success on it. I still have that plaque. Another vivid memory was Coach himself. I could tell that he loved teaching young people. He loved being involved with them and helping them to improve. He loved seeing them advance into adulthood and live successful lives.

"At the end of the week, we all got two photos as mementos of our week at basketball camp. One was a photo of Coach Wooden and me. The other was a group photo of the entire camp—all the campers, counselors, coaches, and staff, along with Coach himself.

"Years later, I became an assistant coach at UCLA. One day when I knew Coach was coming to campus, I took the group photo to show to him. By this time, he was in his early nineties, and two decades had passed since that photo had been taken. But you know what? He knew the name of every single coach at that camp. He had something unique to say about each one."

Why did Coach Wooden remember each coach so clearly after more than twenty years? Because each one was important to him. He loved his coaches and he never forgot them.

Coach Wooden was a leader of leaders, a coach of coaches, a teacher of teachers—and a friend who never forgot his friends.

4

Be a Teacher

Teaching players during practices was what
coaching was all about to me.

Coach John Wooden

John Brooks is CFO of Trinity Classical Academy, a Christian
school in Santa Clarita, California. He told me, "I was growing up
in California, and I was a big fan of all that Coach Wooden accomplished at UCLA. So I was really excited when my dad registered
me for the John Wooden camp as I was going into the ninth grade.

"Coach taught us with a calm demeanor, and he explained
everything with a simplicity and economy of words. He'd say,
'This is what we do, and this is why we do it.' At camp, I received
a special award for my age group. The award included a plaque,
a photo of me with Coach, and a signed copy of his book *They
Call Me Coach*—the first of many Coach Wooden books I've
read over the years. From his camp and his books, I've absorbed

countless lessons that I've applied in raising my sons and in coaching basketball at the Academy.

"After high school, I got my degree from UCLA. I had a campus job and worked in the psychology department. In the later years of his life, Coach sometimes came and lectured on sports psychology. I went to hear him speak one time, and after his talk, I walked down to introduce myself and shake his hand. As it turned out, he was scheduled to talk to another group on campus, so he took my arm—because of his age, he needed a little steadying—and I walked with him to his next event. I ended up being his companion for the rest of his day on the campus, and I got a chance to talk to him and tell him how much I appreciated his influence on my life through his basketball camp.

"Coach Wooden was an incredible teacher. He had thoughtful, insightful answers to every question that was put to him. He recited poetry and Scripture off the top of his head. He communicated wonderful stories and anecdotes to illustrate his principles. If I lived to be a thousand, I would never forget that day.

"I later went into the entertainment industry and worked as a business manager. In 2007, I left the entertainment industry and became the full-time CFO of Trinity Classical Academy, which was founded in 2001. The school started a basketball team, and I served as the first coach. I taught my players lessons I had learned from Coach Wooden at basketball camp, especially the principles of the Pyramid of Success. We played bigger and more established schools, and while we weren't always athletically competitive, many people noticed that we had a different approach to the game than our opponents."

I asked Brooks, "Different in what way?"

Brooks said, "During games, people noticed how our players executed their offense and defense. They saw that our demeanor on the court was different from that of any other team. Our players didn't use bad language, they didn't criticize each other, and they didn't argue with the refs. There was a different spirit out there on the court, and many people from the community, including other coaches, would come to watch our little team play.

"I used many of Coach Wooden's quotes to keep our players focused and motivated: 'Failing to prepare is preparing to fail,' 'Be quick but don't hurry,' and, of course, Coach Wooden's definition of success—"peace of mind, which can be attained only through self-satisfaction in knowing you made the effort to do the best of which you are capable.' I applied that definition to our entire team. As a new, small school, there was a limit to our capabilities, but we were determined to make the effort to be the best we could be. No matter what the final score might be, we had peace of mind that we had done our best. Our players always saw themselves as winners."

I asked Brooks if he remembered any of the practical basketball lessons Coach Wooden had taught him.

"Oh yes," he said. "Absolutely. For example, Coach taught us how to position ourselves to improve our free throw percentage. When they paint the circles on the court, they use a string on a nail that is at the exact midpoint of the free throw line. Coach Wooden taught us to find that nail and position ourselves there so we would always be lined up with the center of the basket. There were a lot of little bits of advice that stuck with me from basketball camp. I passed them along to my players."

I asked, "What about discipline issues? Did you learn important lessons from Coach in how to motivate and discipline your players?"

"I certainly did. I wanted our players to empower themselves and motivate themselves. But one season I had a player who was a very talented athlete, but he would slack off in practice. He was coasting on his talent. He could afford to give a 50 percent effort in practice, and he could still get by on his talent. But his lazy attitude was hurting the team. So I took him aside and said,

'God has blessed you with a lot of talent, which is wonderful for you. But your talent makes you a de facto leader on this team. The other players look up to you as an athlete. They take their cues from you. So you have to be a leader, because they follow your lead whether you like it or not. If you take time off, they'll take time off. They don't have your natural talent, so they can't afford to take time off. And once you start playing against better players, you won't be able to afford it either. So you need to start building good habits now. You have to work harder than anybody else out there.'

"It's the kind of thing I heard Coach Wooden say to players at camp. It worked for him—and it worked for me. That talented young man came back to practice and began working twice as hard as before.

"Coach Wooden inspired me with his example. He was a great teacher, and because of him, I was inspired to be a teacher too."

Focused on the Fundamentals

Swen Nater helped Coach Wooden's UCLA Bruins win two NCAA titles. Though he would have been the starting center on any other college team at that time, he was a Bruin during the Bill Walton era and served as a backup to Walton. In his professional career, Nater was the only player ever to lead both the NBA and the ABA in rebounding.

Born in the Netherlands, Nater came to the United States as a child. He contributed to the Bruins' dynastic record of national titles and went on to play in the NBA with the Milwaukee Bucks, the San Diego Clippers, and the Los Angeles Lakers. He later founded the basketball program at Christian Heritage College in San Diego, where he coached from 1985 to 1995. Nater coauthored a 2006 book with Coach Wooden, *John Wooden's UCLA Offense*.

I asked Nater about his experiences speaking at Coach Wooden's camps. "The guest speakers would come to speak after lunch," he explained. "So the campers would finish their morning activity and go to lunch. The counselors would eat lunch quickly, then go back to the gym for a pickup game.

"The counselors were young, and they liked to show the campers what they could do. So there was usually some dunking, a few behind-the-back passes—all the show-off basketball that runs counter to the fundamentals Coach Wooden taught.

"The guest speaker would speak at one o'clock. I always got there early, and I often participated in those scrimmages. On one occasion, things were getting out of hand, and some of the counselors were showing off their moves, and right in the middle of it, in walks Coach Wooden. He went to the middle of the floor and said, 'Give me the ball.' Then he said to the counselors, 'This is *not* the kind of basketball we teach here. From now on, no scrimmages at lunchtime.' Coach didn't want anyone to undermine his teaching of the fundamentals.

"I was honored that Coach invited me to speak to the campers. Of course, there wasn't much the campers could learn from me because I was six feet eleven and they were four feet eight. I played the post, and none of those campers were able to do that. The only thing I could speak on was post play. So I taught the hook shot and a couple of moves. And I had someone play defense on me so that I could demonstrate some basic offensive skills. The campers got to see a high level of basketball, which was good. But I didn't do anything fancy, because that's not what Coach invited me there to teach.

"I tried to reinforce Coach Wooden's teaching about the fundamentals. But in the Q&A session afterward, the kids would always say, 'Can you dunk the basketball?' That's not what Coach wanted me to teach. So I would lift a camper up to the basket so that he or she could dunk the ball in front of everybody. It was fun, and it gave them a feeling of what it's like to be up there and to throw the ball down through the net.

"But they'd still want me to dunk it. I'd do a straight dunk, just a one-legged takeoff, but the kids wanted me to do a three-sixty, throw it off the board and dunk, and so forth. I did a few of those, but Coach stopped me and said, 'That's not what we teach here. It's better to teach them the different kinds of layups.' I said, 'Okay, Coach.' So he set me straight there.

"Coach Wooden was a teacher," Nater concluded. "He didn't want anything to detract from the pure fundamentals he was trying to teach."

A Hero Who Never Disappointed

"When I was coaching," John Wooden once said, "I always considered myself a teacher. Teachers tend to follow the laws of learning better than coaches who do not have any teaching background. A coach is nothing more than a teacher. I used to encourage anyone who wanted to coach to get a degree in teaching so they could apply those principles to athletics."[1]

Educator and motivator Dave Burgess travels the country conducting seminars for educators based on his book *Teach Like a Pirate*. Burgess told me, "What Coach Wooden said is absolutely true—coaching is teaching and teaching is coaching. You can't separate them. He was first and foremost a teacher. I worked as a counselor at Coach Wooden's camps for three years, from about age sixteen to eighteen. Watching him teach campers the fundamental skills of the game was powerful.

"It was amazing to watch his humility when he interacted with campers and their parents. They'd come up to him and thank him, and they were almost speechless in his presence. Coach would put them at ease. He'd shrug off their praise. By putting people at ease, he made it easier for people to listen to him and absorb the lessons he was teaching."

Greg Hayes told me, "You can learn about basketball from a lot of people, but from Coach Wooden, you learned about life as well as basketball. Listening to him talk about his life, you felt your own life being enriched. He inspired you. He was teaching life through basketball and teaching basketball through life. Once you mastered Coach Wooden's principles for living a good life, it was so much easier to master the principles of basketball. The two reinforced each other.

"Coach was always true to himself, and by being true to himself, he was never untrue to anyone else. The lessons just flowed from his life. His father taught him, 'Make each day your masterpiece.' So Coach did that. And as he made each day his masterpiece, as he loved people and lived out his beliefs, people picked up on that and wanted to be like him. He practiced what he preached, he lived what he taught, and everything he taught was tremendous. In fact, his life exceeded his words. He was a hero who never disappointed."

On Tuesday at camp, Coach Wooden gave his talk on the Pyramid of Success. The Pyramid consists of fifteen principles he identified and refined from 1934 to 1948, when he was getting started as a teacher and a coach. Those fifteen principles formed the foundation of his philosophy of life and his philosophy of basketball.

Craig Impelman told me, "When Coach Wooden spoke at my basketball camps, he'd give his Pyramid talk at the end of the camp. I had campers as old as fifteen, but many ranged in age from six to ten. Coach had figured out that the longest amount of time kids that young would sit still was thirty minutes. So he was determined not to exceed a thirty-minute attention span.

"The first time Coach came to one of my camps, I gave him a glowing introduction that lasted seven minutes. Then Coach got up and spoke for exactly twenty-three minutes. At the time, I wondered why he kept his talk so short. He never said to me, 'Craig, your introduction was too long. Try to keep it shorter next time.'

"I finally figured out that Coach was going to cap his talk at thirty minutes, including my introduction. So if I wanted Coach to have time to talk, I needed to keep my remarks short. I finally got in sync with Coach. I'd say, 'Here's our guest speaker today, John Wooden. He's love and balance.' And that was it. I gave Coach Wooden a twenty-second introduction so the campers would get to hear Coach Wooden for twenty-nine minutes and forty seconds."

Impelman gave me a number of videos of Coach Wooden's Pyramid talks from camps over the years, and I've distilled them into a single message. Picture Coach John Wooden coming out on stage in his polo shirt and shorts. Here, in Coach Wooden's own words, is his presentation of his Pyramid of Success.

John Wooden's Pyramid of Success

"I was raised," he began, "on a small farm in Indiana. My father tried to get across to my brothers and me that we should never try to be better than somebody else. We should try to be the best we can be. Do your best and be your best—that's something you can control.

"I taught high school English for many years, and I tried to get my students to stop worrying about whether they would get an A or a B but to simply make the effort to do the best they can. That might be a C. If you do the best of which you are capable, to me that's an A.

"People tend to judge success based on those who have accumulated material possessions or a position of power or prestige. Now, those are worthy accomplishments, but they are not necessarily successes in my opinion.

"It's like the difference between your character and your reputation. Your reputation is what others perceive you to be. Your character is what you are. You're the only one who really knows your character. You're the only one who really knows if you have made the effort to be the best you can be. "When I began working on the Pyramid of Success, my goal was to formulate a set of principles that would enable me

> *"Do your best and be your best—that's something you can control."*

to become a better teacher. That's all a coach really is, a teacher. I was a teacher of basketball and baseball and tennis, whatever sports the teaching position involved, just as I was also a teacher of English. I worked for fourteen years to develop this concept I call the Pyramid of Success.

"At the very top of the Pyramid is my definition of success, which is based largely on my dad's teaching and which I coined in 1934. My definition of success is 'peace of mind, which can be attained only through self-satisfaction in knowing you made the effort to do the best of which you are capable.'

"In 2003, some friends and I wrote a children's book called *Inch and Miles: The Journey to Success*, and we made the definition of success a bit simpler and easier to remember: 'happiness in your heart is knowing you tried your best.' You can't really be happy unless you know you made the effort to do the best of which you are capable. You can fool others, but you can't fool yourself.

"That's what you should do here at basketball camp. That's what you should do at school. That's what you should do at home, in helping your mom or dad with various household chores and cleaning up your rooms. Always make the effort to do the best of which you are capable.

"That's what you should do in helping others. You can never help another person without truly helping yourself. Helping others is especially important in basketball. When you pass the ball to your teammate, you are helping your teammate, but you're helping yourself. Your teammate will pass the ball to you, and together you will move the ball down the court and score. This principle is equally important in basketball and in life.

"Now, to reach this level of success, this peace of mind, there are certain building blocks you must have in place. I know you'd rather play basketball than listen to an old fellow talk about these character principles, but these principles have been the foundation of my teaching and coaching, and they are the bedrock of those championship seasons at UCLA.

"In this Pyramid, there are fifteen building blocks, and I gave each of these blocks a name. Each represents a personal trait or characteristic you need in order to make the most of the capabilities you have.

"The first block, a cornerstone block, is industriousness. That means hard work. There's no substitute for hard work, and you cannot achieve success without hard work. That's why it's the very cornerstone of the Pyramid. Those who try to take a shortcut and become successful without working for it may get by for a while. But you can't develop the talents within you unless you commit yourself to working hard.

"Then there's the other cornerstone, enthusiasm. You have to enjoy what you're doing. You have to be enthusiastic. You all like basketball, I'm sure, or you wouldn't be here. Am I right? You enjoy playing this game. Your coaches are enthusiastic about it. Your teachers at school are enthusiastic about the subjects they teach, or they should be. Your enthusiasm rubs off on those with whom you come in contact.

"These two cornerstones, industriousness and enthusiasm, anchor the foundation of the Pyramid. They make the foundation strong. They are the first two blocks I chose when I was developing the Pyramid of Success. Over the next fourteen years, I made various changes to the Pyramid, but I never changed the two cornerstones. All five blocks of the bottom tier are essential, but the two cornerstones are the most essential.

"Between the two cornerstones I have three blocks: friendship, loyalty, and cooperation. First, let's look at friendship.

"We all need to work at friendship. Make good friends here, and then make the effort to keep in contact with the friends you make here. In any friendship, both sides have to work at it. If only one side works at friendship, it won't be successful. You have to consider the other person's needs and feelings all the time.

"Then we must have loyalty. You must have someone to whom you can be loyal. And I think you must also have some *thing* to which you can be loyal—a cause, a goal, a commitment. We need both friendship and loyalty if we're to reach our particular level of competency.

"Then we must have cooperation. We need the cooperation of others, and we need to cooperate *with* others. This big world of ours has become smaller because of modern science and technology and the ability to communicate and travel over vast distances. We didn't have jet planes and the internet when I was your age. Not all of these inventions have been helpful, such as the atomic bomb and technologies that create pollution. But if we can control atomic energy for peace instead of war, we can do wonderful things as a society. It all depends on our ability to cooperate with each other.

"The same is true in basketball and in your home. Without co-operation, there is no teamwork, and we cannot succeed without teamwork. You have to work unselfishly with your teammates. You have to work together with your family at home. You have to work together with others in the community. In this troubled world, we need more people working together in a spirit of cooperation. We need more willingness to see the other person's point of view."

Next, Coach Wooden explained the second tier of the Pyramid to his campers. "In the next tier, I have four blocks: self-control, alertness, initiative, and intentness.

"You have to maintain self-control. How many of you lose your temper now and then when you're playing? Do you play better when you lose your temper? Of course you don't. And coaches don't coach well when they lose their temper either. A player or a coach who lets go of his or her self-control is going to be outplayed and outcoached by the team that maintains self-control.

"It's so important to keep your emotions under control. You need to make good decisions. To make good decisions, you must think clearly. Uncontrolled emotions cloud our minds and make it impossible to think clearly.

> *"To make good decisions, you must think clearly. Uncontrolled emotions cloud our minds and make it impossible to think clearly."*

"As players, you need to be disciplined occasionally, because you're young, you're learning, you're inexperienced. When you're learning, you'll do some things incorrectly, and you'll need to be corrected and disciplined. We don't like being disciplined. We all want to think we're ready to compete and we know it all. But we all have room for growth. So we need to be teachable and willing to accept instruction.

"Teachers and coaches need to remember that the purpose of discipline is to correct and improve, not to punish. When we punish, we tend to antagonize. It's difficult to get positive, productive results when we antagonize.

"The next block in the second tier is alertness. Look around you. There's always someone or something you can learn from. Abraham Lincoln once said, 'I never met a person from whom I didn't learn something, although most of the time it was something *not* to do.' Well, that's learning. And you can learn things to do and things not to do by practicing the fundamentals of basketball. But you have to be observant. You have to be alert to the things you can learn.

"Next, you must have initiative. We are imperfect, and we all fail from time to time. That's normal. But if we are afraid to fail, we'll be afraid to start. We'll be afraid to take risks and accept challenges. So we need to have initiative, the willingness to make the attempt, knowing we may fail, but that's okay. The greatest failure of all is the failure to act when action is needed. If we try, we may fail. But if we lack initiative, we are *sure* to fail.

"I've had players who were good shooters but were afraid to shoot for fear they would miss. I wanted them to build up their confidence so they wouldn't be afraid to take the shot. You have to think positively when you take a shot. But I would much rather see that player build up his confidence to shoot when action is needed.

"The fourth block in the second tier is intentness. This means you must be persistent, you must persevere, you must make the maximum effort to reach a desirable goal. Never let hardships or obstacles stop you, because there will always be obstacles along the way. You learn by overcoming obstacles. You never learn by quitting. So persevere and never give up. An anonymous poet once wrote:

> Looking back, it seems to me
> All the grief that had to be
> Left me when the pain was o'er
> Stronger than I had been before.

"We grow stronger through adversity. So keep learning and persevering. Adversity can make you stronger if you accept it and learn from it. Maintain your intentness."

Coach Wooden went on to explain the third tier of the Pyramid. "Now we are coming to the very heart of the Pyramid structure. In the next tier, I have three blocks: condition, skill, and team spirit.

"The next block is condition. Please understand, your physical conditioning must be preceded by mental and moral conditioning.

The order is important. You can't attain the desirable physical condition unless it is preceded by mental and moral conditioning."

"Next, you must have skill. I define skill as 'the knowledge of and ability to properly and quickly execute the fundamentals.' Be sure to work on your physical and mental skills this week. You must be able to execute promptly, to use the proper form in shooting, defending, rebounding, and so on. Learn these skills properly, then practice them repeatedly so that you can perform them quickly, without hesitation or thinking.

"I had some players at UCLA who were great shooters in practice, but they couldn't get any shots in games. They didn't help us at all. I had other players who could get all sorts of shots, but they couldn't shoot, so they didn't help us either. You have to be able to get the shot off quickly *and* accurately in order to get the desired result.

"Quickness is the key to making the most of your skill. Be quick but don't hurry. You must perform that skill in a quick, unhurried way. This is true in both basketball and life. Life often presents opportunities that open unexpectedly and close quickly. We must seize those opportunities before they disappear.

> *"Life often presents opportunities that open unexpectedly and close quickly. We must seize those opportunities before they disappear."*

"A surgeon may have an exquisite skill with a scalpel and the other operating instruments, but those skills are worthless without quickness. When a patient is bleeding or not breathing, a surgeon must act quickly or the patient will be lost. The same is true in business, where you often have to make quick decisions or lose a business deal worth millions. And an attorney who cannot think quickly while questioning a witness could lose an important case. So it's important to have skill—but equally important to apply those skills quickly.

"Next, you must have team spirit. I define team spirit as 'a genuine consideration for others and an eagerness to sacrifice personal interests and personal glory for the welfare of all.' When players have team spirit, they subordinate their own ambitions for the good of the team. And when the team wins, the individual wins as well."

Then Coach Wooden brought his campers close to the summit of his Pyramid. "In the next tier," he said, "I have two blocks: poise and confidence. How do you get poise? How do you get confidence? You get them from the blocks below. If you are building the lower tiers of the Pyramid, you will attain poise and confidence as a by-product.

"What is poise? To me, poise is just being yourself. When you are working or going to school or playing basketball, don't try to be somebody else. Don't pretend you're someone you're not. Be yourself. Poise means you're not pretending, you're not acting, you're not putting on airs. You're just doing your job to the best of your ability.

"To have poise, you must have confidence. If you don't have the confidence to be yourself, you won't have poise. Where does confidence come from? Confidence comes from being well prepared. Failing to prepare is preparing to fail. If you are prepared for success, you'll feel confident and you'll be poised. If you feel unprepared, you'll lack confidence and you won't have poise. That's why preparation is important, and that's why we spend so much time in preparation and drills—so you'll feel prepared, confident, and poised when you play basketball.

"Many people want things to turn out a certain way. They want to be a better shooter or a better rebounder or a better offensive player or a better passer, but they are unwilling to invest time and effort in preparation. They just want the result to happen. They don't want to work for it. Some of you are very gifted athletically, but don't let it go to your head. You need preparation as much as anyone else.

"Remember, success is peace of mind, which can be obtained only through self-satisfaction in knowing you made the effort to do the best of which you are capable. If you have not put forth your best effort, you cannot consider yourself successful, no matter how gifted you may be. But if you have all the blocks of the Pyramid in place, and you've put forth your best effort, you can have peace of mind. You are a success.

"When you have assembled all these blocks together as a foundation, the result will be the last and ultimate block at the apex: competitive greatness. You will be competitive. When you're competitive, you will enjoy a difficult challenge. That's the greatest fun.

"If you play against a little brother or little sister who's not as good as you are, that's no fun. We don't get great enjoyment out of doing things that are easy, the things anybody could do. Joy comes from doing things that are hard. Pleasure comes from overcoming obstacles and adversity.

"Competitive greatness leads us to the apex of success. But you'll notice there are words going up both sides of the Pyramid—ambition, adaptability, resourcefulness, fight, and faith on one side; sincerity, honesty, reliability, integrity, and patience on the other. These are important qualities as well. I couldn't have a block for each of these qualities—that would make the Pyramid too big. So I placed these other qualities along the sides of the Pyramid. Think of them as mortar holding the blocks in place so that the Pyramid remains sturdy and strong. That's how your life should be.

"Let me just say a brief word about the two qualities at the top of the Pyramid: patience and faith. You must have patience as you work hard, build your skills, and prepare yourself for success. All the traits in the Pyramid of Success will make you competitive, providing you have patience. Don't expect success too soon. Good things take time.

"And you must have faith that all things will work out as they should as long as you do what you should. That doesn't mean things will work out as we want them to, but if we have faith, things will turn out as they should.

"We are not all equal with regard to the talents God has given us. Some have greater talents than others. We are not equal in terms of the parents we have, the background we come from, our social and economic status. We are not all the same size. We are all individuals with individual differences. But we can all make the most of what we have. Don't blame others for what you don't have. Be thankful for what you do have.

"Don't blame others for what you don't have. Be thankful for what you do have."

"My dad gave my three brothers and me some basic life principles to guide us. The first one I call Two Sets of Threes:

Never lie. Never cheat. Never steal.

Don't whine. Don't complain. Don't make excuses.

"It doesn't make any difference what other people think. What you think of yourself is the most important thing in the world. Your reputation is what people perceive you to be. Your character is what you really are.

"I could talk for an hour on each block of the Pyramid. I've just skimmed over it a little bit. Keep coming back to the Pyramid in the coming years. Think about these blocks of character and build them into your lives. These blocks will mean more and more to you as you grow older.

"I hope the Pyramid has helped you. I've spent most of my life trying to live up to it. Maybe I'm not all I ought to be and maybe I'm not all I want to be, but I'm better than I would be if I hadn't had something like the Pyramid of Success to guide me and help me to become a better man throughout my life. Young people, I hope you have a real good time this week."

Teaching Basketball and Life

Joe Moore is a novelist and copresident emeritus of the International Thriller Writers. He has authored or coauthored numerous novels, including *Brain Trust*, *The Shield*, and *The Grail Conspiracy*. Moore never played in the NBA and never became a coach—he became a writer, a storyteller. Yet he points to Coach Wooden as one of his most influential and inspirational teachers. He once wrote on his blog:

> One of my heroes is the late UCLA basketball coach, John Wooden. When I was in high school I got to attend his basketball camp, and talk to him a bit. Coach Wooden gave all of us a copy of his Pyramid of Success and taught us more than just the fundamentals of the game. . . .
>
> "I never mentioned winning or victory to my players," Wooden said. "Instead I constantly urged them to strive for the self-satisfaction that always comes from knowing you did the best you could do to become the best of which you are capable."
>
> That's his famous definition of success, and it's rock solid. When we work hard and know we've taken whatever talents we have and pushed them further along, that's achievement. It's one of the reasons I teach writing classes and workshops. I love helping writers get to their own next level, whatever it may be for them.[2]

Moore knows. The teachings of Coach Wooden don't just make you a better basketball player. If you build your life on the Pyramid of Success, you will succeed in any arena of life, in any career path, in any endeavor you set your mind to. If you want to be a novelist like Moore, pay attention to the teachings of Coach Wooden. If you want to achieve competitive greatness in business or media or public service or military service or science or the performing arts or academia, build your life on the Pyramid.

Another writer who attended the John Wooden camps is Matt Lait, a journalist in Southern California. After Coach Wooden passed away in 2010, Lait recalled in an article for the *Los Angeles Times*:

> In 1975, I was an eleven-year-old aspiring NBA player enrolled in John Wooden's basketball fundamentals camp at California Lutheran in Thousand Oaks. . . .
> We were sorted by age into small teams. Wooden would make the rounds as we practiced, offering tips and advice. Twice a day the campers would meet in the gymnasium and Wooden would preach the game's fundamentals and run us through drills. . . . For me, his messages at camp were clear: If you worked hard and were passionate about your pursuits, you could succeed. . . .
> Like many, I found that Wooden's philosophies carried over to all aspects of life.[3]

Craig Impelman shared a revealing insight with me about Coach Wooden's teaching style. "When Coach Wooden came to speak at my camps," he said, "I discovered the key to his approach to teaching: Coach didn't tell you what to think. He made you think for yourself. That was the trademark of all of his teaching at the camps.

"On one occasion, I spoke to the campers about how they should behave when they returned home. I encouraged them to help with the dishes and take out the trash for Mom and Dad without being asked. Then Coach asked, 'What block of the Pyramid does that represent?' The campers raised their hands, and each one came up with a different answer. One camper said, 'That's enthusiasm.' Another said, 'That's team spirit.' Another said, 'That's cooperation.'

"And that's the magic of Coach's teaching. He didn't tell you *what* to think. He made you think. That way you could take the principles he gave you and make them your own.

"I was talking to a basketball coach in Hawaii, a really wise man, and I told him what I had figured out about Coach Wooden's approach to teaching—that Coach made people think. This coach looked at me and said, 'Well, Greg, that's what all great teachers do.'"

He Radiated Wisdom and Love

John Wooden never retired from teaching. He was a teacher until the end of his life. "Whenever I spoke at the camps," Swen Nater told me, "I usually gave Coach a ride back to his condo in Encino. I always had a great time during those drives, talking to him and getting to know him better. I had a little 1971 Volvo that the car dealership had modified for me. They moved the seat back and rebolted it so that, at six feet eleven, I could fit in the car and let out the clutch without knocking my knee against the steering wheel. The car had a nice radio, and I liked to play my music loud. One day when I spoke at the camp, I pulled into the lot and turned off the engine. I forgot to turn off the radio.

"Later that day, Coach and I got in the car to go back to Encino. I turned the engine on, and rock music blasted from the speaker. I turned off the radio and said, 'Sorry, Coach.'

"He said, 'Swen, I've got a question for you. Are you hard of hearing? Now that I look back at when you were on the practice floor, it all makes sense!'"

Swen Nater knew that Coach's gentle ribbing was one of the signs of his love for his former players. He told me another story that illustrated Coach's wise understanding of his players. "After Bill Walton's last year at UCLA, when the Bruins lost in the semifinals, I spoke at the camp. Afterward, I gave Coach a ride home. On the way, he said, 'You know, Swen, we lost the championship, and we should have won it. We were the best team in the country. But I let things get out of control during the year. I got away from the principles I believe in. I let the players have too much say in things. I compromised. And that's why we lost.

"'But I've got a great team right now, Swen. We're not big, but we're quick, and we've got a couple of great guards—the best guard tandem I've ever had. We've got Marques Johnson and Richard Washington, we've got Dave Meyers, and we're a team. I always make a prediction before the season starts of how many wins and losses we're going to have, and I'm rarely wrong. Now, don't tell anybody this, Swen, but we're going to win it all this year.'

"That was in June. At the end of the season, pretty much as Coach had predicted, UCLA had won the title. They didn't win every game—the Bruins went 28-3—but they won the championship game, and then he retired."

Nater told me that Coach was always teaching. *Always.* "He taught me when I was a student at UCLA," he told me. "Coach was still teaching me when I came back and spoke at his summer basketball camps. And he was teaching me one-on-one in our friendship whenever I came to visit him.

"Nell passed away on March 21, 1985, and it was a devastating loss for him. After her death, he used to visit her at the cemetery on the twenty-first of every month. One time I went to visit him at his condo, and I didn't realize that it was the twenty-first of the month. After we had talked for a while, he said, 'Swen, can we go visit Nellie?' I said, 'Sure, Coach.' So we got in my car and started driving.

"I said, 'Okay, Coach, tell me which way to go.' He said, 'You want the directions?' I said, 'Sure.' He said, 'Make a left right here, then make a right on White Oak, then a left on Encino Boulevard. You're going to go three stop signs, then make a right, go up the hill, and it's going to wind past the flower shop. Then make a right on First, and you'll go a little ways, then make a left on Fourteenth, and it's right up there.' I said, 'I'm supposed to remember all that?' He said, 'Well, you asked me for directions.' I said, 'Okay, give it to me again.' He said, 'That's okay, we'll just go.' So he led me turn by turn, and we got there.

"Two months later, I made a point to come on the same day of the month so I could redeem myself. I wanted Coach to know I could follow his directions. So we talked for a while, and—just as I knew he would—he said, 'Is it okay if we visit Nellie?' I said,

'Sure, Coach. No problem. Can you give me directions?' He said, 'No, that's all right.'

"Coach knew exactly what I had in mind. And I asked him later, 'Why did you do that? Why didn't you give me the directions and let me redeem myself?' He said, 'I knew you already learned it.'

"It's like the time Kareem got an A in one of his classes at UCLA. It was a really hard class, and Kareem was proud of himself and wanted Coach to know what he'd accomplished. So he went to Coach and said, 'Coach, look! I got an A!' And Coach said, 'Well, you're supposed to, aren't you?'

"What was Coach teaching Kareem? And what was he teaching me? He was teaching humility. He was letting Kareem and me know that there's no room for ego or elevating yourself or showing how good you are. That's not what life is all about. Life is about helping others to succeed. Do that, and things will work out for you. That's the message he taught his players and campers. That's the message he lived every day. That's the message of the Pyramid.

"Coach strongly disliked individual stardom, and that's why he didn't watch NBA games. He thought the NBA was all about big egos and not about pure basketball. One time when the Lakers were in the play-offs, I visited Coach at his house. I was planning to watch the game and hoping to watch it with him. So as it was getting toward evening, I asked if he was going to watch the game. He said, 'Not if I can help it.'

"I loved spending time with Coach. He just radiated wisdom and love. Coach was always teaching. He taught basketball. He taught life. He taught wisdom, knowledge, and love. He taught on the court and off the court. He never stopped teaching, because he never stopped being who he was."

If you want to learn the lessons of Coach Wooden's life, then study his example. Share your wisdom and love with the next generation. Learn from Coach.

Be a teacher.

5

Teach Wisdom,
Not Winning

What you are as a person is far more important
than what you are as a basketball player.

Coach John Wooden

During the process of writing this book, I spoke to a Saturday
morning session at a convention. I told stories of the meals I had
shared with Coach Wooden and the lessons and insights he had
shared with me. Afterward, a man came up to me and said, "My
name is Steve Danley. I enjoyed hearing you talk about Coach
Wooden. I knew him, and he had a big impact on my life."

"You knew Coach? Tell me about it."

"I was a referee in Southern California for many years. That's
how I became acquainted with Coach Wooden. One day Coach
invited me over to his condo in Encino. It was an amazing experience to sit and talk with him in his own home. He made me feel
special, as if we had been friends for years."

Listening to Danley, I could identify with him. I'd had a similar experience whenever I visited with Coach in his home. I said, "Steve, what's your most vivid impression from your visit to Coach Wooden's condo?"

"Well, this was in 2003, and he had just been awarded the Medal of Freedom by President Bush. I would have thought he'd have the medal framed on the wall or in a display case under glass, but you know where he had it? It was draped over a lamp. I know he felt honored to receive the award, yet it wasn't an honor he wanted to brag about. I guess you could say he didn't want to 'glory' in it, so he hung it on a lamp."

Billy Packer and I were classmates at Wake Forest University. He was on the 1962 Wake Forest basketball team that beat Coach Wooden's Bruins in the consolation game in the NCAA Final Four. Packer had a long career as a college basketball TV analyst and got to know Coach Wooden quite well. Packer once told me, "Coach Wooden is the most humble famous person I've ever met."

Greg Hayes told me that Coach Wooden seemed to radiate wisdom. "At first," he said, "we were all intimidated when we were in Coach's presence. We were intimidated by his reputation, his achievements. I think we all thought, *It's Coach Wooden! The championships, the dynasty, and all that!* But as we got to know him better, the intimidation turned to respect. He went from being Coach Wooden to simply Coach. He didn't seem aware of his own greatness. He seemed to really care about each of his coaches, counselors, and campers. When you were with him, you realized he really cared about you, and it made you feel special. And even after you found out that he made *everybody* feel that way, it didn't take away from how special it made you feel.

"When Coach Wooden walked into the room, there was a kind of spiritual presence there. It wasn't an ego thing or something he projected—his demeanor was always soft-spoken and quiet. He never acted as if he was aware of the high regard we all had for him. He was always so humble and self-effacing. And before the week of the camp was over, our deep respect for him had turned into a love for him. He had that kind of impact on all of us."

I know what Hayes means. Coach had that same impact on me. Recalling the conversations I had with him, I remember the joy I felt just being with him, soaking up his wisdom. I was always impressed by Coach Wooden's humility, gentle wit, and clear thinking. A retired English teacher as well as a coach, he had an amazing memory for poetry and literature and often quoted passages from poets ranging from Shakespeare to Grantland Rice. As I listened to him, totally enthralled, I often thought how wonderful the world would be if everyone was more like Coach Wooden. And at the end of our times together, I always felt my soul had been scrubbed clean.

Coach always inspired me to be a better man. After a couple of hours with him, I wanted to ratchet up my character, my faith, and my wisdom. I wanted to be like him in his simplicity and humility, and I wanted him to be proud of me. Even though I was already a grandfather when I first met him, I felt like he was a father and mentor to me. Years after his passing, he continues to be a big part of my daily life. I continue to study his principles, interview people who knew him, memorize his wise sayings, and measure my life against his.

To this day, I can't get enough of Coach Wooden and his humble wisdom.

Greatest Coach—or Simple Farm Boy?

I've never met anyone as completely unimpressed with his own accomplishments as Coach John Wooden. He must have known what his ten NCAA championships meant in the record books. Yet he didn't even seem interested in the subject. I could never get him to talk about the games and titles he had won. He would simply change the subject. To Coach Wooden, his career had little to do with winning and everything to do with teaching wisdom and character.

Did he care about winning? Intensely so. He truly had the heart of a competitor. But for Coach Wooden, winning wasn't the goal. It was a by-product of character, hard work, practice, and preparation. Coach Wooden was indifferent to his record of wins and championships because humility was so thoroughly ingrained in his soul. He was always self-effacing and always more focused on others than on himself. He never hurried a conversation, never declined a photo or autograph request, and never saw himself as a celebrity.

Greg Hayes told me that the mother of a camper once told Coach, "I'm so happy my son gets to learn from such a famous coach as you."

"Thank you," Coach replied, "but I'm not famous. I've only been in the public eye because I've had the privilege of having so many talented young players under my supervision."

Hayes added, "That wasn't false modesty. That was his genuine humility talking."

Whenever Coach Wooden received a glowing introduction, he deflected the praise with his gentle, self-deprecating sense of humor. Once when Coach spoke at one of Craig Impelman's basketball camps, Impelman introduced him by telling the campers about Coach's many accomplishments at UCLA. After the introduction, Coach stood and said, "Thank you for those exaggerations, Craig—and forgive me, Lord, for enjoying them too much. You know, when you introduce somebody, you're supposed to say nice things, whether they're true or not. Those were some nice things, so thank you. I was invited to speak at an event once, and they wrote it up afterward in the newspaper. The newspaper said they had invited me because they couldn't get an important person. That sort of brings you down to earth a bit."

Coach's story about the newspaper write-up was true. A 1946 edition of the *Elkhart Truth* (Elkhart, Indiana) carried this brief item: "Elkhart school officials announced today that John Wooden, English teacher and coach at South Bend Central High School, would be the principal speaker at their recognition dinner, although they had hoped to get a prominent person."

Leadership author John Maxwell told me he once attended a businessmen's conference where Coach Wooden gave a talk. Afterward, Coach took questions from the audience. Maxwell asked him, "When your life's journey is over, what do you want to be known for?" Coach Wooden replied, "I know it's not the titles and trophies I won." Then he paused a moment. Maxwell told me that

> *"I want it said that I was considerate of others."*

everyone in the audience leaned forward, eager for Coach's answer. Finally, Coach said, "I want it said that I was considerate of others."

Retired basketball coach Bill Oates had a successful career at Saint Mary's College in Moraga, California, and at the Master's College (now the Master's University) in Santa Clarita, California. Oates knew Coach Wooden well. He told me, "Success never changed Coach Wooden. In 2003, he went to the White House to receive the Presidential Medal of Freedom from President Bush. Afterward, Coach Wooden told me, 'I couldn't believe I was there. I am just a simple farm boy.' He remained untouched by all his success."

Every summer Oates drove Coach to Palm Springs to speak at a coaching clinic. "There were about a thousand people there to hear him speak, and he always received a ten-minute standing ovation. Even when Coach was in his nineties, he'd sign books and photos for people for three hours after he spoke. Who else would do that? People had tears in their eyes when they approached him. They were awed to be in the presence of a legend. He had a love for people, so he made himself accessible to all of them. When I drove him home, he was exhausted and his hand was cramped. But he just wouldn't let anyone down."

The world knew John Wooden as the winningest coach of all time, but Coach Wooden called himself a simple farm boy. And he meant it.

Gail Goodrich, who played for Coach Wooden and helped the Bruins win their first two national championships (1964 and 1965), shared an insight with me that speaks volumes about the character and humility of Coach Wooden. "When I was at UCLA," he said, "we played in Arnold Gym on campus. At that time, scholarship players had to do 250 hours a year of work. So every day before practice, all the scholarship players took push brooms and swept the gymnasium floor. And every day Coach John Wooden was out there with us, broom in hand, sweeping the floor alongside us."

He was Coach, and he was a teacher. He was a simple farm boy, and he was the greatest coach of all time. He was a leader, and he was a humble servant. And he was all these things because of the depth of his love and the depth of his wisdom.

The Wisdom to Admit Mistakes

One way Coach exemplified wisdom was by readily admitting mistakes—and immediately rectifying them. Steve Patterson was a six-foot-nine center for Coach Wooden's Bruins from 1968 to 1971. He later went on to play five seasons in the NBA. I've often felt that Patterson deserved more credit for sustaining the Bruins' championship tradition in the years between Lew Alcindor and Bill Walton. Shortly before Patterson's death due to cancer in 2004, I spoke with him about his college career at UCLA.

"I love Coach Wooden," he told me. "But there was a time while I was at UCLA when I was ready to quit the team. I had a bad habit of holding the ball down low where it could get stolen, and

Coach was always getting on me about it. He was right, but he got after me so much that it was hard to concentrate, and I kept making mistakes. One day at practice, he got after me again, and I just couldn't take it anymore. I stormed off the court and headed for my locker. I was actually in tears, and I was seriously thinking about quitting the team.

"While I was standing there in front of my locker, Coach came in. I didn't know what he was going to say, but the last thing I expected was an apology. He said, 'Steve, I'm sorry. I see now that I was too hard on you. I really care about you, and I want you to be the best you can be. But I went too far, and I hope you can forgive me.'

"That was incredible. It meant so much to me that Coach would be humble enough to apologize. That kept me going. That made me love the man all the more.

"That was in 1971. We went on that year to win another title, beating Villanova. I got twenty-nine points in that game, my career high. I hate to think what I might've missed if I had quit that year. And I might've quit if Coach hadn't come into the locker room to say, 'I'm sorry.'"

It takes humility and wisdom to admit you were wrong. In 1962, Coach Wooden's Bruins made it to the first round of the Final Four but lost to Cincinnati by a mere two points. Coach blamed himself for the loss.

"When UCLA qualified for the NCAA postseason tournament," he reflected, "I intensified our already grueling practices, working players even harder—so hard, in fact, that by tournament time they were physically and mentally spent. . . . I added new plays and piled on more information. Instead of staying with what had worked during the regular season—a clear and uncomplicated strategy—I intentionally made things complicated. I resolved that in the future I would keep it simple going into postseason play just as I did during the regular season."[1]

111

Coach Wooden had learned the lessons of failure. Two years later, his Bruins won their first NCAA title.

Craig Impelman told me about another time Coach admitted he'd made a mistake. "Coach had a lot of wise sayings," Impelman said, "and you can find them in his books and on the internet. But there is one widely quoted saying that Coach later wished he hadn't said. It goes like this: 'Politeness and courtesy are a small price to pay for the goodwill and affection of others.' One day Coach said to me, 'Craig, I don't like that quote, and I don't use it anymore. Politeness and courtesy are not a price to pay. Politeness and courtesy are just the basic consideration we should give to everyone we meet, simply because it's what we ought to do.'"

The ability to admit mistakes and change course is a key ingredient of leadership. And it's a sure sign of wisdom.

The Wisdom of Selflessness

Gary Williams is a former college basketball coach, a university administrator, and a network basketball analyst. He recalled an unexpected act of kindness that Coach Wooden did for him in 1978. "I got the head [coaching] job at American U," Williams said. "I wrote [Coach Wooden] a letter . . . asking for some material that he had on full-court pressure. He sent me back a handwritten two-page letter concerning his 2-2-1 press, which I still have. I was flabbergasted. I'm sure he didn't know who I was, and he took the time to draw some diagrams on it and things like that, which I'll never forget."

Williams framed Coach's letter, hung it on his wall, and points to it with amazement and pride, adding, "He says, 'Young man, you've picked a great profession. Respect the profession. Always do as good a job as you can. But never forget the players playing for you. John Wooden.' How 'bout that?"[2] That's exactly the kind of help and kindness Coach showed to so many people throughout his life.

Former UCLA forward Jamaal Wilkes told me, "If there is one principle that really sums up John Wooden's life, it would be helping others. His example has impacted me greatly. When you help others, you don't do it expecting anything in return. You just help people because it's the right thing to do. Yet it always seems to work out that when you help other people, you help yourself as well."

Craig Impelman echoed Wilkes's words. "Helping other people was what Coach was all about. He treated everybody great—not just good, *great*. He took a personal interest in everybody he met. It didn't matter if you were young or old, a king or a pauper, rich or poor. Coach would always take an interest in you, and if there was anything you needed, anything he could do for you, he'd gladly do it. It wasn't something he put on. His love for others flowed from his heart. He was the most remarkable individual I've ever known.

"When Coach would come to speak at my camps, we always made time for people to meet him, take a picture, or get an autograph. The first couple of years we did this, Coach would end up sitting there for three hours. There were so many people who wanted to talk to him, and each one had a story to tell him or a question to ask. Many of them brought T-shirts or sweatshirts for Coach Wooden to sign—usually while they were still wearing them. Coach would have to pull the shirt out straight so that he could write a good, legible signature, and that was time-consuming. Obviously, three hours is too long for Coach and too long for the people in line. I decided something had to be done.

"So one year I set up some guidelines and printed them up in a handout that went to all the campers and their parents. In that handout, I said that it takes too long for everyone to engage Coach Wooden in a five-minute conversation, so please just say hello, get your photo or autograph, and keep the line moving. And please don't ask him to sign your shirt.

"So on the last day of camp, Coach came to speak, and we had this policy in place. And after his talk, I got up and reminded the campers and their parents that they could come up and greet Coach Wooden—'but please don't ask him to sign your shirt and please help us keep the line moving.' Well, Coach was sitting behind me with his black Sharpie in his hand. And the moment I finished my speech to the campers and parents, he smiled, gave me a little wink, and said, 'Lean over for a moment.' So I leaned closer to him, and right in front of everybody, he grabbed my T-shirt and signed it across the front, 'Best wishes, Coach Wooden.'

"The audience laughed, and Coach said, 'Okay, honey, you'd better go give them the rules now.' Well, with a stroke of his Sharpie, he had canceled the rules. He had a mischievous sense of humor, and that was his way of telling me that he had come to make himself available to people for as long as they wanted. And that included signing T-shirts."

I asked Impelman why people were so drawn to Coach Wooden. After all, he didn't come across as a dynamic speaker, yet people loved to listen to him speak. "It was his wisdom and love that drew people," Impelman said. "Coach Wooden's love for people attracted everyone to him—especially young people. I remember being with Coach at a children's birthday party, a party for an extended family member at a Chuck E. Cheese's pizza place. There were a lot of youngsters, most of them preschoolers or kindergarten age. Now, they didn't have any idea who Coach was. They didn't know anything about his years at UCLA or his string of championships. He went over and sat in a chair against a wall and watched the children play.

"But after a while, I looked over at Coach and saw that he had eight or nine children gathered around him. They were sitting at his feet, and one was on his lap, and they were just fascinated by him. And he was smiling at them and talking to them, and the kids were drawn to him. Well, that's just the good spirit and loving nature of John Wooden—it shone from him and drew people in. Children seemed to be especially receptive.

"And you know what? He had the same impact on the young people at his camps. They were drawn to him because of his genuine love for them. Most of the campers were too young to be fully aware of his reputation. They had some idea that he was famous because their parents had told them so. But the campers weren't attracted by his fame. They were attracted by his love for them.

"One of the most important influences he had on them was the way he modeled wisdom, love, and humility. Most of the role models in the sports world are people with big egos and flashy personalities. But Coach Wooden showed a generation of young people that it was cool to be caring and humble. He showed them that you could be famous and highly accomplished without being a show-off.

"Talk to the people who went to those camps and ask them what they remember about John Wooden, and they'll tell you how he treated everybody great. They'll tell you they remember his caring. They'll tell you they remember his humility. And they'll tell you that his example has stuck with them ever since."

I asked Impelman if he remembered any incidents or stories about Coach's impact on the lives of his campers. He said, "I do. Let me tell you a story. Once during our summer basketball camps, the mother of one of the campers came up to me and said, 'What are you teaching at this basketball camp?' I was a little taken aback by the question. I said, 'Well, we're teaching Coach Wooden's ideas and principles, as Coach himself taught them, and we're teaching basketball fundamentals.'

"She said, 'Well, let me tell you what happened. My son Ryan is nine years old. Last night I was in the kitchen, and I had taken out a big glass punch bowl. I was going to use it to make something up for company. But I dropped the bowl, and it crashed and broke. Shattered pieces were all over the kitchen floor. Ryan saw it happen, and he saw how upset I was. So he came over to me, put his arm around me, and said, "Mom, don't worry about things you can't control, because it's going to take away from the things you can control. I'll help you clean this up." And he got a broom and dustpan and helped me. Now tell me—where did he get *that* from?'

"I said, 'That came straight from Coach Wooden.'

"That's the kind of influence Coach Wooden had. He was always influencing others that way, everywhere he went. I sometimes went with him to a restaurant or the grocery store, and no matter where he went or who he talked to, he always tried to make their day a little better. There were times when I knew he wasn't feeling good physically, but he never complained. Instead, he always tried to help *other* people feel better."

I asked Impelman what Coach was like as a leader at the camps. "He was always positive. At the basketball camps, there was a big staff and a lot of campers, and everything was supposed to happen right on schedule. From time to time, things went wrong, but I never heard Coach Wooden complain about anything, not once, not ever.

"In fact, there are a lot of 'never' statements you can make about John Wooden. And *never* is a strong word. Yet I can honestly say I *never* heard Coach Wooden interrupt anybody. Never. Even if a lady in line was telling him a long, boring story about when her grandson played basketball at UCLA, he would *never* interrupt.

"I *never* heard John Wooden say a negative word about anyone. Never. I *never* saw John Wooden treat anyone less than great. I *never* saw John Wooden be unprepared. I *never* knew him not to follow up on a promise he made. If he told you he'd do something, he did it. If you said, 'Coach, would you please mail a Pyramid of Success to my brother in Oklahoma?' he'd say, 'Give me his name and address, and I'll send it off today.' And Coach would go home that day and mail out the Pyramid with a nice letter—without fail.

"Helping others was his trademark. More than any other trait, Coach Wooden's love for others defined who he was and what he was all about."

Swen Nater shared a related insight with me. On one occasion, Nater was traveling with Coach Wooden and his daughter, Nan. At one point in their trip, Nan asked Nater to go to the hotel and pick up Coach and help him with his luggage. So Nater drove to the hotel, went up to Coach's room, and knocked on the door. Coach opened the door and said, "Could you give me about five minutes? Come in. You can wait in the room."

So Nater went into the room and watched as Coach tidied up the room to make less work for the maid. He took the used filter out of the coffee machine and placed it in the trash. He took the towels he had used and neatly folded them on the counter. He tidied up the bed. Then he left a five-dollar tip for the maid.

Why did he do that? He wasn't trying to set an example. He was just treating people with kindness. He was showing that he cared. He was being Coach Wooden. That's the kind of person he was, and he didn't know any other way to be.

I saw Coach treat people with kindness when I was with him as well. When we were at a restaurant, I saw him engage waiters and busboys in conversation, asking them questions and listening intently to their answers. I saw him have conversations with strangers in the parking lot and with neighbors at his condominium complex, not polite chitchat but real conversations. He was genuinely interested in everyone he met. He genuinely loved people. He genuinely cared.

The world needs more people like John Wooden. The world needs more people who are committed to helping others.

The Wisdom of Self-Control

Los Angeles Times writer Mike Faneuff attended a Wooden basketball camp for four years, from 1968 to 1971. One of his most vivid memories of the camps was Coach Wooden's insistence that his campers and coaches exhibit the character trait of self-control. Coach Wooden, Faneuff wrote, "never swore, and didn't tolerate it from us. If we continually messed up a drill, he'd holler 'Goodness gracious!' or 'Sakes alive!' If he got really angry, it'd come out all together: 'Goodness gracious sakes alive!'"[3]

Craig Impelman observed that Coach Wooden's insistence on self-control had as great an impact on the coaches at the camps as it did on the campers. "John Wooden felt that profanity showed a lack of self-control," Impelman told me. "And you can't be successful if you can't control yourself.

"And consider this. The Cal Lutheran campus in Thousand Oaks was also the training campsite for the Dallas Cowboys. Coach Wooden's campers not only had Coach himself as a role model but also had Tom Landry, the Christian coach of the Dallas Cowboys. The campers and the coaches got to see two coaching legends—Coach Wooden running his basketball camp and Coach Landry running his football camp—and both of them exemplified self-control and clean speech. What a great example for the young coaches at the basketball camps to see. What great role models, demonstrating how to instruct and motivate their players in a positive way.

"A number of years ago, I was doing a basketball coaching clinic in La Crescenta, north of Los Angeles. I was teaching John Wooden's principles to people who were coaching youth basketball, grades two through seven. I was teaching John Wooden's lessons in love and balance just as I had learned them from him. After one session, a young coach came up to me, a guy in his early twenties. He wanted to talk privately.

"'Coach Impelman,' he said, 'is it true that John Wooden was never mean to his players and never used bad language?'

"'That's right,' I said. 'He was instructive, he was direct, but he was never mean or harsh. And not only did he never use profanity himself, but he would not permit his staff or players to use profanity.'

"'Oh, that's great news!'

"'What do you mean?'

"'Well, when I was growing up, my coach always swore at us. He was mean, and he motivated us by intimidation and punishment. I thought that if you were a coach, you had to be harsh and you had to swear at them.'

"'No, Coach Wooden was the winningest coach of all time, and he never did that.'

"'That's great! If Coach Wooden could accomplish what he did without swearing and without intimidating his players, then I know it's okay to coach that way.'"

It's true. Coach Wooden became the greatest coach of all time by pointedly *not* screaming, *not* swearing, and *not* intimidating his players. He preached self-control. But even more important, he *lived* it.

Former UCLA forward Jamaal Wilkes recalled, "Coach didn't spend a lot of time preaching to us about God, but his actions always spoke louder than his words. I was with him every day for three years at UCLA and never heard him swear. He was intense and competitive, but he always maintained his self-control. I think that's because his life was truly controlled by God. He trusted God to be in control of his circumstances, so he never worried about the things he couldn't control."

Influencing Others, the Wooden Way

Greg Hayes told me, "I can't go a day without doing, thinking, or saying something I learned from Coach. Whether I'm teaching in the gym or on the field or in the classroom, I'm constantly using insights and lessons I learned from Coach. Wherever I go, whatever

I do, his voice is in my head. His influence continues to impact my life. And Coach continues to impact other people through me and through the other people he mentored.

"The longer I live, the more I realize that to understand the depth and richness of John Wooden's thoughts, you really have to experience life. A lot of what Coach tried to teach me didn't make sense when I was younger. It takes time and experience to appreciate his wisdom.

"Coach never said those words with a lot of emotion. He was soft-spoken. But the depth and the power of his words, and the way he backed them up by his example, could change your life. He didn't just say things to whip up our emotions. He became the greatest coach of all time by living those words in the real world. You always felt you could become a better human being and a better athlete by following his wisdom."

Longtime *Los Angeles Times* sportswriter Bill Dwyre told me what he experienced while researching and writing a feature story on Coach. "I spent seven or eight long interview sessions with him," Dwyre said, "and when I finished, I was in a deep depression." Why a deep depression? Because Dwyre didn't want the interviews to end. He wanted to continue his conversations with Coach. He said, "I thought, *I can't go back because I have enough material, but I miss the man.* John Wooden makes you want to be a better man."

I know that feeling well. I, too, never wanted to leave him when our time together was over. He had that kind of impact on campers, counselors, and coaches.

The winningest coach of all time wasn't impressed with winning. He was obsessed with wisdom. There's no better way to teach, no better way to coach, and no better way to live your life than the way of wisdom—the Wooden way.

6

Empower Your People

Young people need models, not critics.

Coach John Wooden

Coach Wooden invited many of his top UCLA players to speak and demonstrate technique at his camps. One of those players was Jamaal Wilkes. During his UCLA career, he was known as Keith Wilkes. He took the name Jamaal after he began playing for the Golden State Warriors. But to Coach, Jamaal would always be Keith—old habits die hard—and Wilkes understood and accepted it.

When Wilkes spoke to the campers, Coach Wooden introduced him with these words: "I'm often asked to describe the perfect college basketball player. And I'll say, 'He has to be a good student, quick to learn. He has to be polite and courteous, completely unselfish, and willing to pass the ball. He has to be quick on the floor and a good team player. He should be a good defensive player and a strong rebounder. He should be a good inside player and a good outside shooter. In short, my definition of the perfect college basketball player is Keith Wilkes.'"

Wilkes was standing in the back of the gym listening to his old coach give him this glowing introduction. He had never heard Coach Wooden say any of this before, and hearing those words brought tears to his eyes. He had to step out of the gym for a few moments to compose himself.

Those words from Coach Wooden were an incomparable gift from a coach to a player, from a teacher to a student, from a mentor to a learner. Coach Wooden was an encourager and an empowerer. And he continued to empower his players long after they left his supervision. Coach Wooden believed that the way to help people achieve more is by building up their confidence, not tearing down their self-esteem.

Greg Hayes described Coach Wooden to me this way: "Coach didn't dish out a lot of verbal praise, and he never handed out false praise. If you got a verbal compliment from Coach Wooden, you knew you had earned it. Coach had his own way of showing his approval, and the campers picked up on it right away. You could hear it in his tone of voice. You could see it in his expression and in his eyes."

Not only did Coach Wooden teach the Pyramid of Success to his players and campers, but his approach to coaching was also intended to encourage the fifteen traits of the Pyramid in the lives of the young people he coached. Whether he was coaching college players at UCLA or campers at his basketball camps, he was constantly encouraging young people to build their lives on a foundation of industriousness, friendship, loyalty, cooperation, enthusiasm, self-control, and all the other traits of the Pyramid. A young person whose life is built on this foundation will be, by definition, *empowered*.

One of the ways Coach Wooden empowered his campers was by making sure every practice ended on a positive and uplifting note.

He never ended a practice with criticism, always with a word of encouragement or a motivational poem. He made sure his players never criticized one another but always encouraged one another. Coach believed in the maxim "Treat everybody great—not good but great!"

Though focused on positive empowerment, Coach did not hesitate to correct his players, campers, counselors, and coaches

"Treat everybody great—not good but great!"

when they needed it. But no one ever felt punished or shamed. Coach Wooden surrounded all of his correction with affirmation. As Greg Hayes told me, "If Coach gave you a word of instruction, you might feel corrected, but you never felt criticized or condemned. He never intimidated. He always inspired."

Coach Wooden treated campers as if they were his UCLA players. He taught them the UCLA high post offense and put them through the same up-tempo drills he had used with his championship teams. During the drills, campers clapped out the tempo, just as Coach Wooden's players had done back in the day. Coach had the same expectations, the same team rules, the same high level of instruction that had been the norm during the dynasty years at UCLA. As much as humanly possible, those campers got to experience what it was like to be on one of Coach Wooden's great Bruins' teams.

What young camper wouldn't feel as tall and powerful as Bill Walton or Lew Alcindor while learning from the greatest coach of all time?

Creating Confidence

Sports broadcaster Lynn Shackelford played basketball at UCLA for Coach Wooden. He told a story that illustrates Coach Wooden's genius for empowering his players to achieve more than they ever thought possible. During his freshman year at UCLA, Shackelford was a 75 percent free throw shooter. One day Coach approached him at practice and said, "You know, Lynn, I think you could be a much better free throw shooter than you are. During games, you make almost every jump shot from the same spot, but you're making only three out of four free throws. I have a suggestion. Instead of taking time to bounce the ball before your free throw, just step up to the line and shoot. Don't think about it—just do it."

Shackelford took Coach Wooden's advice. He later recalled, "I was over 80 percent for most of the next year."[1]

Coach Wooden knew that confidence was a huge factor in performance. Confidence is near the top of the Pyramid of Success and is one of the two main supporting blocks of competitive greatness.

One way Coach Wooden built confidence on his UCLA teams and on his camp teams was by employing the "pointing rule." Whenever a player scored off a pass, that player was required to point to the player who had made the assist. The scoring player had to point to the assisting player until they made eye contact. That gesture conveyed thanks to the assisting player and was a way of sharing credit for the basket.

Sharing credit is a powerful way to empower your players and encourage unselfishness. No one ever shared credit more unstintingly than Coach Wooden. Sports columnist Adrian Wojnarowski recalled a visit to Coach Wooden's condo:

> To insist to Wooden what most sensible sports minds consider fact—that he's history's greatest coach—invites a disapproving grimace, an understanding that he isn't interested in contributing to such a consensus. Wooden rises to his feet and instructs a visitor to walk with him to a mantel, insisting, "I want to show you something." He grabs a small wooden box, flips back the lid and cups a bronzed medallion in his hands. An award the Big Ten

delivered him as a Purdue graduating senior in 1932, representative of the top student-athlete in the conference.

"It's my most prized accomplishment," Wooden says, "because only I was responsible for it. All the coaching awards, I had just a small part in them. Those belonged to my players. . . . This, though, I was responsible for earning."[2]

When Coach deflected credit for his coaching accomplishments, when he claimed he had just "a small part" in all those championships, he was not merely being humble. He was following his own "pointing rule" and thanking his players. He was giving them the credit—and he was empowering them.

Just as Coach insisted on his players sharing credit for team accomplishments on the floor, he also insisted that players never criticize or attack one another. Greg Hayes told me about an incident at one of Coach Wooden's camps. During an afternoon game, Coach watched as an older boy made a perfect pass to a younger teammate on a two-on-one fast break. The younger player went up for the easy layup—and *missed*.

The older boy was furious! He proceeded to yell and berate his teammate, breaking a cardinal rule of the camp. One of the camp coaches pulled the offender out of the game and sat him on the bench.

Moments later, Coach Wooden strode to the bench and looked reprovingly at the boy. "Goodness gracious," Coach said. "The young man you were yelling at is your teammate. You won't build his confidence that way. I expect you to be more supportive of all your teammates and help them to have a good experience at this camp."

"Yes, Coach," the chastened player replied. "I'm sorry."

Coach Wooden's "goodness gracious" was all the boy needed in the way of reprimand. From then on, he was a model of team spirit and empowerment.

Empowering without Words

Tarik Trad, a community activist in Los Angeles, attended a John Wooden basketball camp at Point Loma College near San Diego in 1976. The cost was $200, which was a lot of money for his family. But Trad's father thought the experience was important enough for him to make the financial sacrifice. The cost covered five days of instruction, room and board, a camp jersey, a pair of basketball shoes, and photos with Coach Wooden and two of Coach's former players, Marques Johnson and Swen Nater.

Trad recalled that on game days there were eight basketball games going on at the same time. Coach rode from one game to the next on a golf cart driven by the head counselor.

During a game that Trad was playing in, he happened to make a difficult shot over an older, taller, more-skilled player. Moments later, Trad stole the inbounds pass and made another tough shot over the same defender. Best of all, Coach Wooden saw it all.

Coach stepped out of the golf cart, walked over to Trad, and winked. He didn't say a word to Trad. He didn't have to. That wink said it all. Then Coach climbed back into the golf cart and went on to the next game.

It was a lot harder for Trad to score after that. All the other players wanted to shut down the kid who had gotten a wink from Coach Wooden. But Trad never forgot that moment of empowerment he received from basketball's greatest coach.

Years later, Trad's wife happened to be reading some books on leadership and management techniques. She asked Trad if he had ever heard of something called the Pyramid of Success. She had no idea who John Wooden was, nor that he had led UCLA to ten NCAA championships. She had a birthday coming up, so Trad contacted Coach Wooden's office to see if he could get an autographed copy of his latest book for her. He wasn't sure if Coach Wooden—who was almost ninety-five at the time—still honored such requests.

But a few days later, the book arrived in the mail, inscribed by Coach Wooden and addressed to Trad's wife. The inscription concluded with the words, "Make each day your masterpiece. Coach Wooden."[3]

The same Coach Wooden who empowered a young camper with a wink in 1976 was still empowering people through his acts of kindness in the closing years of his life. That's the way I want to live my life—always encouraging others, always building confidence in others, always empowering others.

Giving People Room to Be Themselves

Coach Wooden was an equal-opportunity empowerer. He didn't empower just the campers. He didn't empower just the counselors and the coaches. He empowered *everybody* who was involved in making the camps a success. That included the kitchen staff. When Coach Wooden's camps were held at Cal Lutheran in Thousand Oaks, meals were provided by the school's director of food services, Lil Lopez, and her staff of fifty cafeteria workers.

Greg Hayes told me that Coach remembered the name of each of those cafeteria workers, and he frequently talked to them about their families, their hopes and dreams, and their work at the camp. He thanked them for their contribution to the lives of his campers. He took a genuine personal interest in each worker. And there was nothing more empowering than receiving that kind of personal attention from Coach himself.

Coach Wooden made it clear to his counselors and coaches that he expected them to follow his example and empower the campers. Greg Hayes recalled one session Coach had with his coaching staff in which he reminded them, "It's amazing how the youngsters' hearing improves when they hear praise and encouragement from their teachers."

Keith Glass told me that Coach Wooden had a way of sharing ideas and suggestions with his coaches without telling them how to implement those ideas and suggestions. Coach was a good delegator, and he wanted to empower his coaches to make their own decisions, as long as they achieved his overall goals for the camps.

"One of the great joys of driving Coach Wooden," Glass said, "was that I got to ask him every question under the sun. I asked him questions about the game of basketball, about coaching, about life. And he would answer my questions with examples from his own experience. He explained how he coached his players, how he conducted his practices, how he implemented his strategy, and so forth. He talked very openly with me, and I got quite an education.

"But he never said, 'You have to do it my way.' He would tell me how he did it, then he would always conclude with, 'Now, Keith, that's how I like to do it, but it's not the only way. You might find another approach that works better.' He always wanted to give his players and coaches room to be themselves. But when I listened to his advice, I'd always think, *This is the guy who's won ten NCAA titles. Of course I'll do it his way.*"

Stories of Empowerment

After Coach Wooden passed away in 2010, his writing partner, Steve Jamison, set up a Memory Wall page at the CoachWooden .com website. Scores of people posted tributes to Coach, including many who had been impacted and empowered by him. Here are a few of those stories.

Several people recalled calling Coach at home, seeking just a few minutes of his time, and they were astonished that Coach invited them to his condo for visits lasting hours or even all day long.

One man who had lost the ability to walk because of a stroke found himself sitting next to Coach on a two-hour airline flight.

Coach Wooden told the man that if he put his mind to it, he just might overcome his disability and be able to walk again. Inspired and empowered, the man underwent three years of physical therapy and regained the power to walk.

One young man posted that he asked Coach Wooden to autograph his Bible. A surprised Coach Wooden said, "Oh no, I don't sign Bibles! That's God's Word!" But this young man had nothing else to autograph, so Coach finally said, "Just this once I'll make an exception." He took the Bible, wrote a personal note on the flyleaf, and signed it, "Best wishes, John Wooden—1 Corinthians 13."

My favorite anecdotes on the Memory Wall came from people who attended Coach Wooden's summer basketball camps. A mom recalled sending her teenage daughter to a Wooden camp. The young lady had tried out for basketball but had failed to make the cut. The disappointment was hard on her self-esteem, but the camp boosted her confidence. "Coach selected my daughter as camper of the week," the mom concluded. "He changed my daughter's life, and she is now a pediatrician."

A young man who attended Coach's camp at Cal Lutheran recalled, "One morning we were running the UCLA offense (or trying to), and I had just made a pass from the high post when Coach happened to be walking by. He commented on how well we were running the offense. I was grinning the rest of the day. Coach Wooden had seen my play!"[4]

Ann Meyers Drysdale was the first woman to receive a four-year athletic scholarship to a university. She played on the UCLA women's basketball team from 1974 to 1978. She is also the only woman ever to sign a contract to play in the NBA (a $50,000 no-cut contract with the Indiana Pacers in 1979; she participated in tryouts but was not selected for the final roster). Ann is the younger sister of Dave Meyers, who played college basketball at UCLA for Coach Wooden (he went on to play four seasons with the Milwaukee Bucks). Ann was married to Baseball Hall of Fame pitching legend Don Drysdale until his death in 1993.

Coach Wooden became acquainted with Ann when her brother Dave was a leader on UCLA's 1975 NCAA championship team—the last UCLA team John Wooden coached. Ann sometimes spoke and coached at the Wooden camps. Though some of the camps were for boys only, others had both boy and girl campers. Coach Wooden wanted the female athletes in his camps to have positive role models to look up to and emulate. A five-foot-nine, blonde, blue-eyed point guard, Ann Meyers Drysdale gave the girl campers a fine example to follow. Like many members of Coach's own family, she called Coach by the nickname Papa.

"I loved going to Cal Lutheran to work in the summer," Drysdale told me. "Whenever I think of Coach Wooden's camps, wonderful memories come flooding back—the weather, the smells, the excitement of the Dallas Cowboys being there. I was shy and quiet, but Papa had a way of teasing me and making me laugh so I would feel confident and comfortable.

"Picture day was one of my favorite events. The campers would get their pictures taken with Papa. They were all so excited, and he was so patient with them, giving each camper a smile and a word of encouragement to make them feel special. So many of those campers are now grown men and women who have gone on to be great parents, great businesspeople, great leaders, in large part because of those summers at the basketball camps."

Drysdale and Coach Wooden formed an enduring bond as learner and mentor. In her book *You Let Some GIRL Beat You?*, Drysdale recalled:

Papa used to say that the importance of basketball was small in comparison to the total life one lived, and that the only kind of life that truly won was a life that placed itself in the service of others and in the hands of God. His love of UCLA had more to do with the friendships he made there, and for that reason he could often be found on campus walking the track or just hanging out in his office long after his coaching days.⁵

Debbie Haliday is program assistant for UCLA women's basketball. She told me about attending a John Wooden summer basketball camp for girls. "I attended the camp when I was sixteen," she told me. "Though it was an all-girls camp, I never felt Coach Wooden treated us any differently than the guys. I always felt he respected our game and enjoyed watching us play. He talked to us as athletes. At the end of each practice, he would give us a quiet word of encouragement or motivation. He told me once that I was a pure shooter and I should keep shooting the ball when I'm open. That made a big impact on me as a young player.

"I played basketball at UCLA, graduating in 1982. I got to know Coach Wooden better after I graduated and began coaching. He became a mentor and friend and was much like a wise and caring grandfather to me. His encouragement probably had a lot to do with my decision to go into coaching.

"In 1991, I was the head women's basketball coach at Biola University. As a young, first-time college head coach, I was trying to lay a foundation for the program. I couldn't think of a better way to do that than by going through the Pyramid of Success. We worked our way through each block of the Pyramid, and the impact on my players was immediate. Coach Wooden's principles are so good, so right, and so powerful!

"It occurred to me—why not ask Coach himself to teach these principles to my team? I wrote him a letter and gave him my phone number. To my surprise and joy, he called me and said he'd love to spend time with my team. He spent two hours with my athletes, teaching them the principles of the Pyramid, answering questions, reciting poems, and telling stories. My players were amazed, and so was I.

"One time after Coach and I had breakfast together, I drove him back to his apartment. I said, 'Coach, I hope you have a great day!' He said, 'I intend to.' His optimistic reply has stuck with me all these years. Whenever I'm not feeling particularly positive going into a day, I hear his voice in my head reminding me that the way my day goes is largely determined by my attitude and my intentions. If I *intend* to have a great day, I probably will.

"There are so many messages Coach has given me that replay in my thoughts again and again. 'Be quick but don't hurry.' 'If you don't do it right the first time, when will you have time to do it over?' 'Pay attention to the smallest details.' 'Do something every day for someone who can't repay the deed.' Coach had a way of taking the truths of the Bible and making them practical and clear. He showed you by example what it looks like to live a righteous life."

I recently heard the story of another young woman Coach Wooden encouraged and empowered. Her name is Kelly Schaefer.

In the summer of 1999, nineteen-year-old Schaefer was vacationing with her family and her boyfriend in Colorado when the car she was riding in was struck head-on by a drunk driver. Schaefer was left paralyzed—a quadriplegic. In her memoir *Fractured Not Broken*, cowritten with Michelle Weidenbenner, Schaefer tells the story of how she recovered her will to live by devoting her life to serving and inspiring others. As she began making public appearances and inspiring audiences with her story, her principal role model as a public speaker was Coach John Wooden.

> *"If you don't do it right the first time, when will you have time to do it over?"*

Though Schaefer was a devoted basketball fan (especially the basketball program at Indiana University, where she had been a cheerleader), she knew little about Coach Wooden's achievements as the UCLA coach. But someone had recommended his Pyramid of Success to her, and the principles of the Pyramid had clicked into place for her. His ideas all made sense, especially his definition of success, which she memorized: "peace of mind, which can be attained only through self-satisfaction in knowing you made the effort to do the best of which you are capable." As a quadriplegic, Schaefer had physical limitations on her capabilities, but she still had her mind, her voice, and her indomitable spirit, and she was determined to do her best with those abilities.

At one of her speaking events, someone took a picture of her holding a copy of the Pyramid of Success. That photo found its way to Coach Wooden, and a short time later, Schaefer received a letter from Coach himself and a copy of his Pyramid of Success, which he had inscribed as follows:

> *For Kelly—with congratulations on your positive out-look. Why—we can't understand, but we must believe in who directs our path.*
>
> *Best wishes,*
> *John Wooden*

When Schaefer's stepfather saw the letter and the Pyramid of Success, he looked at her in astonishment and said, "Do you know who this guy is?"

Though Kelly was a devoted basketball fan (especially the basketball program at Indiana University, where she had been a cheerleader), she knew little about Coach Wooden's achievements as the UCLA Buins coach. So she got on the internet and researched Coach Wooden's career—and then she was truly in awe that he had taken the time to write to her with a message of empowerment.

"Although I'd never met him," Schaefer reflected, "his words inspired me. . . . He'd influenced many people in his career. Could

I do the same? Could I be a person with all the attributes on Mr. Wooden's Pyramid? I wasn't sure, but I wanted to try."[6] She studied and meditated on one of Coach Wooden's quotations: "Things turn out best for those who make the best out of the way things turn out." In 2004, she entered the Ms. Wheelchair Indiana competition—and won. The title gave her a bigger platform for encouraging others and advocating on behalf of people with disabilities. She was profiled in the *Herald* of Jasper, Indiana, and a copy of the newspaper article reached Coach Wooden.

A few days later, another letter appeared in her mailbox:

Dear Kelly,

A mutual friend of ours recently sent me a copy of the article concerning you that was published in The Herald. You truly are a most remarkable young lady and exemplify the words of the one who said, "God never closes one door without opening another."

We never know where our paths may lead, but must have faith in the one chosen even though we may never understand the reason why. Adversity will make us better and stronger if we accept it without bitterness. As our great President Abraham Lincoln said, "If we magnified our successes the way we magnify our disappointments, we would all be happier."

May enduring peace between all nations in this troubled world and true love for one another among all people become a reality in our time.

Sincerely,

John Wooden[7]

Coach Wooden knew there is no greater way to live than living to empower others. He empowered players and coaches and campers. He empowered the sportswriters who interviewed him.

He empowered a basketball player named Ann Meyers Drysdale. And he empowered a courageous young lady named Kelly Schaefer to transform her wheelchair into a vehicle of healing, hope, and inspiration to countless other people.

That's how empowerment works. That's how empowerment spreads from one person to another to another, radiating outward like ripples on a pond. There's no greater way to live, and no more effective way to love, than by empowering the people around you.

> *"Adversity will make us better and stronger if we accept it without bitterness."*

7

Strive for Competitive Greatness

Don't measure yourself by what you have accomplished but by what you should have accomplished with your ability.

Coach John Wooden

John Wooden was hired as the UCLA Bruins' head basketball coach for the 1948–49 season. The previous season the Bruins had posted a losing record of 12-13. Under Coach Wooden, the Bruins underwent an instant turnaround, achieving a 22-7 record and the Pacific Coast Conference (PCC) Southern Division championship. Despite this dramatic and immediate turnaround, the Bruins didn't achieve the first of ten NCAA Division I championships until 1964—almost sixteen years after Coach took the job at UCLA.

Coach later reflected, "Somebody asked me—'You know, how come it took you so long to win a national championship?' And I said, 'I'm a slow learner; but you notice when I learn something, I have it down pretty good.'"[1] Yes, ten championships later, Coach clearly had it down pretty good.

If ever one human being epitomized competitive greatness, it was John Robert Wooden.

Ironically, many people today have an aversion to the very notion of competition. "What the world really needs," they say, "is not more *competition* but more *cooperation.*" They mistakenly equate competition with cutthroat aggression, unprincipled ambition, ruthless antagonism, and other negative traits. Yet while Coach Wooden was the ultimate role model of competitive greatness, there was nothing cutthroat, unprincipled, or ruthless about him. In fact, his concept of competitive greatness is the very capstone of his Pyramid of moral qualities.

> *"I'm a slow learner; but you notice when I learn something, I have it down pretty good."*

It's impossible to imagine anyone more principled than Coach Wooden—and it's impossible to imagine anyone more intensely competitive. Is that a contradiction? Absolutely not. Competitive greatness, as Coach Wooden defined it, is not only consistent with good character but also requires it. You can't achieve competitive greatness without good character. His definition of competitive greatness is inscribed on the uppermost block of the Pyramid of Success:

COMPETITIVE GREATNESS
Be at your best when your best is needed.
Enjoyment of a difficult challenge.

You don't need good character to be aggressive, ambitious, or ruthless. But true competitive greatness, as Coach Wooden defined it, can only be built on a foundation of strong character traits—the building blocks of the Pyramid of Success. Coach Wooden did not win ten NCAA titles through ruthlessness and aggression. He achieved that unparalleled level of success by focusing all his teaching, coaching, and influence on two essential themes:

1. Strengthening the moral conditioning, mental conditioning, and physical conditioning of his players through the Pyramid of Success.
2. Building the competitive skills of his players by keeping them relentlessly focused on the fundamentals of the game.

By doing these two things, Coach Wooden achieved a seemingly impossible goal—a goal that is unlikely ever to be equaled. He spent his life striving for competitive greatness, and he achieved it—and then he spent the rest of his life teaching the fundamentals of competitive greatness to succeeding generations.

John Wooden demonstrated his competitive greatness by always giving 100 percent of himself to every camp he conducted. He could have simply lent his name to the camp, shown up for an hour to deliver a pep talk, then headed for the exit. Many sports celebrities have done exactly that. But Coach Wooden strove for competitive greatness in everything he did, including the John Wooden Basketball Fundamentals Camp. He was there every day, giving the talks, teaching the skills, conducting the drills, offering individual instruction where needed, teaching the Pyramid, and impacting lives. His name was on the camp. He made it special.

Today, many of Coach Wooden's campers look back and say, "My life was changed by my encounter with true competitive greatness."

The Heart of a Competitor

If you ever had a conversation with Coach Wooden, you could have easily gotten the wrong impression about him. You could have come away from your encounter thinking of John Wooden as merely a gentle-natured, soft-spoken, Midwestern high school teacher who liked to quote poetry. If you hadn't known who he was and what he had accomplished, you never would have imagined that the heart of a fierce competitor beat within his chest.

If you asked him about the games his teams had won or the championship banners hanging from the rafters at Pauley Pavilion, he waved your questions aside and changed the subject. If you heard him speak about the Pyramid of Success, you heard a lot about hard work, friendship, cooperation, and self-control and not a word about winning.

You might have gotten the impression that winning simply wasn't important to him. And you would have been wrong. Oh boy, would you have been wrong.

Though he never swore and never violated his values and principles, Coach was a Bruin in every sense of the word—a fierce, competitive grizzly bear. If he felt the officiating was unfair, Coach would harangue them and try to keep them honest. In fact, he readily admitted it. "Oh, yes," he said. "I'd try to work them. I'd say things like 'Don't be a homer,' or, 'Call them the same at both ends.'"[2]

Retired NFL official Jim Tunney officiated UCLA basketball games during the Wooden era. "John would get on us plenty," Tunney recalled. "I remember during the Alcindor years, he'd yell, 'They're killing Lewis in there, they're killing him.' . . . But I do have to say I never heard him utter a cuss word. Not once. That wasn't always the case with some of his assistants, however."[3]

Not only would Coach work the referees, but he'd also heckle opposing players if he thought they were getting away with cheating or roughing his boys. He recalled, "I'd do that to try to get them thinking about you, hoping it would get them off their game."[4] Some opponents were shocked to discover that the seemingly mild-mannered Coach Wooden could exhibit such intense competitiveness. One stunned USC player told a reporter after a game, "You wouldn't believe what Wooden was yelling at me out there." As Wooden biographer Steve Bisheff concluded, "You can't be the great coach that he was without also being a great competitor."[5]

Unlike so many coaches who prowled the sidelines like caged beasts, Coach Wooden did all his haranguing from his chair—and he rarely got out of that chair and rarely said a word to his own players. Bill Walton recalled, "He had that famous rolled-up program—we never knew what was in it, because he never called a play, never called time outs. He'd say: 'Men, I've done my job; the rest is up to you. When the game starts, don't look to the sidelines, because there's nothing I can do for you.'"[6] Coach felt that if he moved from his chair or barked orders to his team, doing so would shake their confidence. The only people he spoke to from his chair were refs and opposing players.

In all his years as a coach, John Wooden received only two technical foul calls from officials—and one of those, he insisted, he didn't deserve. The official thought he'd heard Wooden say something he never said—and never would say.

Torey Lovullo was eleven years old when he attended one of Coach Wooden's camps at Pepperdine University in 1976. Years later, he told an interviewer about a lesson Coach taught him—a lesson about competitiveness. "I'll never forget the day I was playing in a scrimmage game," Lovullo said, "and Coach Wooden saw me stop the game so I could re-tie my shoes. He pulled me off the court and said, 'Young man, never ever tie your shoes during a game. Make sure you double-tie them so you don't give your opponent an advantage by resting and catching up.'"

In 1985, Lovullo again encountered Coach Wooden—this time at a fried chicken restaurant. By that time, Coach had been retired for a decade, and Lovullo was in his sophomore year at UCLA. "I was in my UCLA uniform," Lovullo recalled, "and I heard an elderly gentleman behind me ask, 'Did you win your game today?' I turned and recognized Coach Wooden immediately. I answered, 'Yes, we beat USC.' He looked pleased to hear the news. Then he said, 'Don't ever forget that those four letters across your chest should mean something to you. You beat those Trojans every chance you get.' I wish I had seen him again so I could tell him we beat USC thirteen straight games, starting with that game."[7]

Coach Wooden's competitive nature even imposed limits on his willingness to help one former player. Henry Bibby was a starting point guard for Coach Wooden's Bruins and was a key factor in three consecutive NCAA titles—1970, 1971, and 1972. Bibby also helped power the Bruins through the first forty-seven games of their phenomenal eighty-eight-game winning streak. Yet when Bibby was named head basketball coach for the USC Trojans, Coach Wooden drew a line and refused to cross it. Yes, he would give Bibby advice over the phone, but he refused to visit his former star player on the USC campus.

Bibby recalled, "He would say, 'Henry, you are one of my boys, but I will never go watch you coach over there.' He was UCLA through and through."[8]

Coach Wooden and his Bruins dominated college basketball throughout the 1960s and into the 1970s. During his twenty-seven years at UCLA, Coach Wooden won back-to-back NCAA championships in 1964 and 1965. The Bruins fell short in 1966 but came back to run the table year after year for seven years, 1967 through 1973. After a disappointment in 1974, Wooden and his Bruins won a tenth championship in 1975, then Coach retired. Not a bad record of accomplishment for a fellow who saw himself as a high school English teacher.

To top it off, Coach Wooden racked up all those titles with an assortment of teams. It's only natural that fans remember the mega-talented Bruins of the Lew Alcindor and Bill Walton years. Yet Coach also won titles without players of the size and caliber of Alcindor and Walton. Wooden's first national championship team, the 1964 Bruins, didn't have a starter over six feet five, and his final championship team in 1975 was similarly undersized.

Coach Wooden's record of accomplishment was not the result of size and talent, though Coach Wooden would be the first to give the credit to his highly talented players. He was able to win with big men and big talent, but he also won with far less impressive rosters. Why? Because he focused on character and conditioning and the fundamentals. Above all, he focused on competitive greatness.

Little Things Add Up

Coach Wooden was intensely focused on all the little details that added up to a competitive edge. When I asked him to pinpoint one secret of success in life, his answer was a lot of little things done well. He knew that all those little details added up to a big competitive advantage over your opponents. He knew that those tiny little details were where individual games and entire championships were won or lost. That's why he was so focused on such matters as how a player put on his socks and shoes or how long a player's hair was.

Many of Coach Wooden's UCLA players assumed that Coach's rules about hair length and clean-shaven chins were due to the fact that Coach was an old fogey from Nowheresville, Indiana, whose sense of style was stuck somewhere in the Great Depression. But one of Coach's players eventually figured out that Coach Wooden's rules were all about winning. Years after Keith Erickson graduated from UCLA, he discovered why Coach Wooden made his players keep their hair short. "That was because," Erickson said, "if you perspire and run your hands through your hair, the next time someone threw you a pass, the ball could slip through your

Success Is in the Details

hands. That happened to me years later in a game [in the NBA] and I realized, 'Doggone it, that's the reason.'"[9] Coach Wooden schooled his players and campers in the fine points that easily went unnoticed. By the final buzzer, those fine points often added up to a winning difference. One example was his oft-repeated fast-break wisdom: "You'll never have a better chance of getting an offensive rebound than when you take a jump shot at the end of a break—so take it." Another detail Coach Wooden emphasized in practice was that his players should always practice free throws after a heavy workout; that way, they'd be practicing free throws while their muscles were tired from exertion, simulating conditions in a game.

These are all little details, too insignificant to matter, right? Yet Coach Wooden insisted that these "insignificant" details were the key factors in his ten NCAA championships. How can we argue with success?

These little things are the key to simplicity, the key to preparation, the key to achieving our goals, the key to maintaining a consistent level of excellence, the key to building good habits every day, and the key to guarding our character against moral weakness and failure. Life is all about the little things, and those who achieve great success in life pay careful attention to the little things. "Develop a love of details," Coach once said. "They usually accompany success."

One of the most important ways Coach Wooden paid attention to the little things was in the way he treated others. In 1977, one of the campers at his summer basketball camp at Pepperdine University was a seven-year-old boy named Will Moselle. Looking back on his limited skills at that age, Will told me, "When shooting free throws, I could barely get the ball to the hoop."

During the camp, Will liked to go to the outdoor court before breakfast to practice his free throw shooting. One morning, Coach Wooden was taking his morning walk by the court and noticed Will shooting and missing, shooting and missing.

"Coach came over," Will told me. "He spent several minutes with me, working on my shooting form. I'm amazed to think back on it. The greatest coach in history took time to give private instruction to me, a seven-year-old kid."

After high school, Will attended UCLA and served as student manager for the Bruins basketball team under head coach Jim Harrick. One day, Will was in the hallway next to Coach Harrick's office when Coach Wooden stopped by. Coach had been retired for years, but loved coming back to campus to talk to the coaches and students. "Coach engaged me in conversation about school and sports for about ten minutes," Will told me. "Then Coach Harrick came out of his office and said, 'Coach Wooden, come on in!' Coach said, 'Just a moment. Let me finish my conversation with Will.' By saying that, Coach conveyed to me that I was no less important to him at that moment than the head basketball coach at UCLA. That meant a lot to me."

It was a small gesture, but it made a huge impression on Will Moselle. Coach Wooden always acknowledged people, always treated everyone with respect, kindness, and attention, whether he was talking to a homeless person on the street or the President of the United States. Everybody was important to John Wooden. Kindness and acknowledging others is one of the little things he did to make a big difference in the lives of the people around him.

Life is made up of little things, simple things. By focusing on these small details, we prepare ourselves to produce consistent high levels of performance and excellence. Great achievements are the result of striving for perfection in the seemingly minor details. Little things make big things happen.

A Moment of Illumination

The sports world first witnessed John Wooden's competitive greatness in action during the early 1930s, when he played basketball for the Purdue Boilermakers under Coach Ward "Piggy" Lambert. Johnny Wooden played with a competitive intensity that wowed Purdue fans and stunned his opponents. He gave 100 percent on every play, sacrificing his body, diving headlong for loose balls, and earning such nicknames as the "Indiana Rubber Man" and the "Human Floorburn." Often, while diving for the ball, he'd go flying into the stands. The fans would pick him up, turn him around, and launch him back onto the court. As Coach Wooden later recalled with a grin, "I went down on the floor a lot."

Young Johnny Wooden led the Boilermakers to conference championships in 1930 and 1932 (the latter year posting a near-perfect record of 17-1). While Wooden was on the Purdue roster, the Boilermakers posted a record of 42-8.

After college, Wooden took a position as an English teacher and coach at South Bend Central High School in Indiana and played semipro basketball on the weekends. He played for three teams and once set a phenomenal record of 134 consecutive free throws as a player for the Indianapolis Kautskys (named for the team owner, Frank Kautsky). Wooden later recalled that after he made the hundredth consecutive free throw, Kautsky came out onto the court, stopped the game, and handed Wooden a $100 bill. Wooden sustained that streak over a span of forty games.

As a player, Wooden used a free throw style that has almost completely disappeared from the game—the granny-style approach of launching underhand from between the legs. From 1965 to 1980, Rick Barry (Golden State Warriors, Houston Rockets) amassed a .900 free throw percentage (best in NBA history) using that same technique.

Ever the competitor, Coach Wooden sometimes challenged his UCLA players to a free throw contest. The players all used the standard overhand form. Then Coach Wooden went to the line, lowered the ball between his knees, and launched it toward the basket. Nothing but net. He proceeded to school his players in the art of the granny shot. If any of them were laughing at the beginning of the demonstration, they weren't laughing when it was over. The old man still had it.

The granny shot was tailor-made for Coach Wooden's philosophy of balance and fundamentals. The standard overhand free throw form is asymmetrical, making it easy for a shot to veer left or right. The two-handed granny shot is perfectly symmetrical. As long as your throw is neither too strong nor too weak, the ball should find the hoop. It's interesting that Coach Wooden never taught granny-style free throw shooting to his players. Perhaps he thought it would be too hard for them to unlearn the style they had been taught in high school.

In March 1975, Coach Wooden and the Bruins squared off against his former assistant Denny Crum and the Louisville Cardinals in the NCAA semifinal game. In overtime, the Cardinals led 74 to 73 and had possession of the ball with ten seconds remaining. Crum put free throw specialist Terry Howard in the game. When the Cardinals inbounded, UCLA was forced to foul Howard, who hadn't missed a free throw all season. Howard stepped to the line, and Coach Wooden burned his last time-out to ice him. It worked. Howard launched the ball—and it rattled out. UCLA rebounded and got the ball to Richard Washington, who hit a jumper with three seconds remaining. UCLA won, 75 to 74.

Coach Wooden's emotions churned following that win. As a competitor, he was thrilled for himself, his players, and the UCLA community. But he knew it was a devastating loss for his friend Denny Crum. "I couldn't help but feel awful for him," Coach said later. "As I walked across the court to do the postgame television interview, the thought crossed my mind for the first time. I thought, *Now's the time to quit.* I'm not exactly sure why I thought it at that moment, but I did. I went into the locker room and I told my team that I was as proud of them as any team I had ever coached, that they had listened well all season and had been a joy to teach.

Then I said to them, 'I can't think of a better group to have worked with as the last team I'll ever teach.'"

He wasn't sure that his players had picked up on what he was saying. But he went out to the postgame press conference and made the announcement that he was retiring after the final game—and the reporters were stunned. "I knew it was the right thing," Coach reflected, "because as soon as I said it, I felt satisfied and pleased."[10] His Bruins went on to defeat Kentucky for the national championship—his tenth—and Coach Wooden retired at the age of sixty-three.

Why did Coach come to such an abrupt and final decision just moments after winning that game? To my knowledge, he never really explained his thought process that night. Maybe he couldn't, because he didn't fully understand it himself. I think I have a good guess. I think Coach realized something after defeating his friend Denny Crum. He felt awful for Denny, and he shouldn't have. He realized that winning that game would've meant so much more to Denny than it did to him. Denny had no banners hanging in the rafters of his arena. Coach Wooden was about to add his tenth.

Perhaps when Coach realized that his love and caring for his friend and former assistant was overtaking his competitive intensity, he knew it was time to retire. He knew it would be harder to work up that kind of intensity for an eleventh banner or a twelfth. He knew that sustaining his competitive greatness was only going to get more and more difficult. If he had defeated any other coach that night, the idea of retiring might not have occurred to him. But he had defeated Denny Crum in a game that easily could have gone the other way—and he'd felt awful about it.

That was a moment of illumination. That was a moment of insight.

So Coach retired after ten championships, and he moved on to the next stage of his life. He became a teacher, mentor, and coach to thousands of young campers. He taught new generations of young people how to strive for competitive greatness.

Confidence Is Contagious

Greg Hayes recalled a lunchtime conversation between Coach Wooden and his coaches at a Cal Lutheran camp. As the counselors and campers were heading to the gym for free time, one of the coaches asked Wooden, "How do you develop confidence in players?" "Confidence," Coach Wooden replied, "comes from being prepared and being successful every day in practice. Failing to prepare is preparing to fail. . . . Build competitive greatness through teaching better skills."

Then Coach talked about one of UCLA's greatest games—the game against Denny Crum's Louisville Cardinals, the game at which he made up his mind to retire. "In the 1975 semifinals against Louisville, [Richard Washington] made the shot at the end to win the game for us because he was confident and was not afraid. It was not going to ruin him if he missed that shot, because he was confident he wasn't going to peck the shot and shoot short. . . . The coach should convey a feeling of confidence."[11]

In other words, the best way to build confidence in a player is by making sure that player is thoroughly prepared and knows you believe in him. The top block of the Pyramid is competitive greatness, which rests on two supporting blocks, poise and confidence. Poise is just being yourself. Confidence is the result of being prepared and keeping everything in perspective.

"The coach should convey a feeling of confidence."

With three seconds left to play, his team trailing by one, Richard Washington had the ball—and the game—in his hands. A confident player loves to be in that situation. A player who lacks confidence is terrorized by those clutch situations. Coach Wooden wanted his coaches to understand how to build the confidence of his campers so they would have the confidence and competitive intensity to always want the ball when the game is on the line.

He also wanted his coaches to radiate confidence. Fear is contagious, but so is confidence. If you believe in your players, they'll believe in themselves. Confident players are at their best when their best is needed. They enjoy a difficult challenge. In his camps, Coach Wooden always looked for ways to prepare his campers, increase their skills, grow their confidence, and intensify their competitive greatness.

Literary agent Steve Laube attended a John Wooden–Bill Sharman basketball camp in Honolulu in the summer of 1974 (Bill Sharman was then the head coach of the Los Angeles Lakers). Laube recalled that he and his fellow campers were drilled and instructed during the day, then they scrimmaged in afternoon and evening games.

In the course of one drill, Coach Wooden pointed at young Laube and said, "Come here, young man, and show me how you rebound the ball."

So in front of the other campers, Coach Wooden took young Laube to school and showed him how to box out. Coach Wooden was a sixty-three-year-old man at the time, and Laube was a lanky, athletic teenager, about seventeen years old. "No matter what I did," Laube recalled, "spinning, pushing, hip-checking, and jumping, he always snagged the rebound. I couldn't believe this gray-haired 'old man' who was at least five inches shorter than me could do that. . . . It was only later that I found out that he was in the Hall of Fame . . . as a player (inducted in 1960)! No wonder he taught this skinny kid a lesson."

Even though Coach Wooden had Laube beat at every turn, he was careful not to undermine the camper's confidence. At the end of the demonstration, Coach clapped Laube on the back and said, "Good work, son."

Laube reflected, "He didn't shame me, he didn't show me up. He taught me and everyone else on the court the power of good footwork, dogged determination, and that you didn't have to jump high to get every rebound. The memory of that is so strong I can still feel his elbows, hips, and other bones grinding into my thighs and ribs as I tried to get around him."[12]

The lessons Coach taught that teenager in 1974 stood him in good stead in his later years. Laube didn't become a professional athlete, but his confidence and his striving for competitive greatness took him far in the publishing field, first as an editor with a major publishing house and later as the founder of a successful literary agency.

To Be a Winner, Don't Focus on Winning

UCLA women's basketball coach Cori Close recalled that throughout her mentoring relationship with Coach Wooden, he would make her think, but he would never tell her *what* to think. "I would ask for his advice, and he would say, 'Oh, no, I don't share advice, I only share my opinion. . . . You can't coach like me or anybody else. You need to coach within your own personality, and find your own vision.' . . . The freedom he gave me to be my own person is remarkable."

One of the most important lessons Close learned from Coach Wooden is how to strive for competitive greatness by *not* focusing on winning. "Coach Wooden won his first few championships without a lot of talent [on his teams]," she said. "His ability to adjust and get the Lew Alcindors, the Bill Waltons, [enabled him] to continue that sustained excellence. One of his keys was, he never looked at it through the eyes of winning or outscoring the opponent. He never talked that way."

She observed that Coach Wooden placed the goal of competitive greatness "at the top of his Pyramid of Success for a reason. You really never talk about it. It's a by-product of building that Pyramid with incredible attention to detail, and commitment to the foundation, and all those other things. . . . [Winning] doesn't really need to be spoken of. It happens when you build those kinds of habits, and you get to the top of your building process."

Close applies Coach Wooden's wisdom and his Pyramid of Success to her own life and to the lives of the student athletes she coaches. "I've tried to take that approach with this program," she said. "Don't get distracted by outscoring opponents, or recruiting battles, or things that are not true measures of whether I'm being the best coach I can be for this team. . . . Some of my colleagues have said, 'Well, that must mean that winning isn't that important to her. Listen to the way she talks.' But I just don't think you talk about it. The same habits that lead to winning basketball games are the same ones that make you a great teammate, that make you a great employee, that make you a great leader."[13]

Wooden never talked to his players about winning. It was as if the word *winning* wasn't in his vocabulary. Coach Wooden knew that you don't win by focusing on winning. You win by focusing on acquiring the traits of competitive greatness—the building blocks of the Pyramid of Success. And you win by mastering the fundamentals of the game. If you do those two things well, you'll never have to talk about winning. You'll never have to think about winning. Oh, you'll win all right. Winning will be a by-product of perfecting the skills and attributes of competitive greatness. Coach knew that all his players had to do was play to their full potential, and they would walk off the court as champions.

Coach never screened game film, never scouted his opponents. He never saw any need to. He insisted that if his players mastered the fundamentals and prepared themselves to play their own game, they would never have to worry about what their opponents might do.

And he was proven right.

We don't achieve competitive greatness by focusing on winning. In fact, the best way to strive for competitive greatness is by putting winning completely out of our thoughts. Instead, we should strive to lay the building blocks of the Pyramid of Success in our lives, block by block, tier upon tier. It starts with industriousness, friendship, loyalty, cooperation, and enthusiasm, and it continues through poise and confidence. If we have the first fourteen building blocks of the Pyramid properly laid in our lives, the fifteenth and uppermost block, competitive greatness, will naturally fit into place. That is what Coach Wooden taught his championship teams at UCLA. That is what Coach Wooden taught his campers in the summer camps at Cal Lutheran and Pepperdine and Point Loma and Honolulu. And that is what Coach Wooden is saying to you and me today.

There's a very good reason why the capstone of the Pyramid of Success is competitive greatness. That should be the goal not just of every athlete but of every human being on the planet. Competitive greatness is not selfish ambition or ruthless aggression. Competitive greatness simply means performing at our best when our best is required—and as Coach Wooden would be quick to remind us, our best is required each day.

Build a life worth living. Build with building blocks of good character traits that lead to poise and confidence. Build a life that produces competitive greatness in everything you do.

Do that, and you'll know the true meaning of success, which is peace of mind, which comes from knowing you did your best when your best was needed. And your best is needed every day.

8

The Undiscovered
Coach Wooden

Love is the medicine that can cure all the ills
of the world.

Coach John Wooden

Ralph Drollinger was a seven-foot-two center who played for Coach
Wooden at UCLA. He was taken in the NBA draft three times but
chose to forgo the money and fame of pro basketball, choosing
instead to play on a traveling evangelistic basketball team, Athletes
in Action. He eventually signed with an NBA expansion team,
becoming the first signed player in the history of the Dallas Mav-
ericks. He later became a pastor, author, and TV producer as well
as a world-class mountaineer. Drollinger once said, "Character is
the basis of leadership, and Coach Wooden had it. His character
was impeccable."[1]

Drollinger founded Capitol Ministries in 1997, an organization
that fosters Bible studies for political leaders in Washington, DC,

and in state capitals across the nation. He told me that his entire career—from professional sports through his present ministry of providing spiritual leadership to our nation's leaders—can all be traced back to a single summer basketball camp he attended while in high school.

"As a junior in high school in San Diego," he told me, "I was fortunate to win a scholarship to a Wooden summer basketball camp in Pacific Palisades. The first day of camp I dislocated a finger on an outdoor court rim. Coach Wooden reset the dislocated finger himself. That's how I first met him. I thought he was not only a great coach but a great doctor as well.

"A year later, Coach called me and said, 'Ralph, you are one of three players we have decided to recruit this year.' At that point, Coach Wooden's Bruins had won eight of their eventual ten NCAA championships. How could a youngster say no to such a legend as Coach Wooden?

"Because of that summer basketball camp, I later became the first player in history to play in four consecutive NCAA Final Fours. My college basketball experience set the course for the rest of my career and my present ministry. I can never thank God enough for the privilege of having John Wooden as my coach and mentor."

Mike Krzyzewski, head basketball coach at Duke University, once said, "Many have called Coach Wooden the 'gold standard' of coaches. I believe he was the 'gold standard' of people." And one of Coach Wooden's favorite UCLA players, Jamaal Wilkes, said, "It wasn't until years later, after college, after the NBA, when my life focus began to change on marriage, divorce, children, the business world, that I began to sense how special a man he was."[2]

Bill Walton made a similar observation. "I had no idea what we had at UCLA," he said. "I thought everybody had the same thing: great parents, great schools, great neighborhoods, great colleges, great coaches. Then I joined the NBA. And I realized immediately that I had just absolutely blown this whole deal with

John Wooden. . . . All the things that [Coach Wooden] said turned out to be true. When he was telling us, we were like, 'This is the stupidest stuff ever.' Pyramid of Success? Seven-Point Creed? Two Sets of Three? But then he'd say, 'Do your best, your best is enough. Whatever you do, don't beat yourself, don't cheat yourself, don't short-change yourself. Because you'll never get over it.' And we had no idea what he was talking about."[3]

> *"Whatever you do, don't beat yourself, don't cheat yourself, don't short-change yourself."*

Walton first met Coach Wooden in the early 1960s at—you guessed it—a summer basketball camp. It wasn't a John Wooden Basketball Fundamentals Camp—those didn't begin until 1971. But Coach Wooden spoke at a camp at the University of San Diego when Walton was about ten years old. Walton got to shake Coach Wooden's hand, and at the time, it was as if young Walton had touched the hand of a legend.

Later, after Walton had shot up to become a six-foot-eleven center for UCLA, he began to take his old coaching hero for granted. Walton gave Coach Wooden a lot of what he later called "consternation." Walton never defined that word, but I got the impression it was composed of one part heartburn, one part bellyache, and one part grief.

During one of the Q&A sessions for campers and parents at a Wooden basketball camp, a camper asked Coach Wooden about an incident involving Walton: "Is it true that you benched a player because he wouldn't cut his hair?"

Coach smiled. "That was Bill Walton," he said, "one of the truly great players in the history of the game. And it's true that I *would* have benched him if he hadn't cut his hair and shaved. After Bill's sophomore year at UCLA, he was picked as player of the year. We had won a national championship and had an undefeated season, and he thought he was pretty good. He knew

I had certain requirements for our players, but he didn't think he should have to follow them.

"Now, I wouldn't allow long hair or facial hair, and I had good reasons for those rules. I believe that long hair and facial hair act like a blanket. They trap heat and cause perspiration that can get in your eyes and make it hard to perform well on the court. An excess of perspiration can trickle down and make you uncomfortable and cause you to make errors.

"After his sophomore year, Bill reported for the first day of practice with long hair and a beard. He said, 'Coach, you don't have the right to tell me how to wear my hair.' And I said, 'Bill, you're absolutely right. I don't have that right. However, I do have the right to determine who's going to play—and I'm going to miss you.'

"He went right out and got a haircut and a shave, and that was the end of that."

"We Had No Idea"

Bill Walton later looked back on his college years with both fondness and regret—fondness because of the privilege he had to play for Coach Wooden and regret that he didn't appreciate Coach more at the time. "I was his worst nightmare, his biggest challenge and biggest failure," Walton told an interviewer. "The maddest I'd ever seen him was the day he came to bail me out of jail after a peace rally at UCLA." Police had arrested Walton and fellow protesters for lying down in the middle of Wilshire Boulevard to protest the war. Coach paid fifty dollars out of his own wallet to set Walton free.

"Driving me home, he was in my face," Walton recalled. "'How can you do this? How can you let everybody down?' I told him, 'Coach, I have friends coming back from Vietnam in body bags.' He told me I was right about the war, but I was going about it the wrong way, that I should write letters."

Walton thought about it, then decided to take Coach Wooden's advice—sort of. He went into Wooden's UCLA office and took some of Coach's letterhead stationery. Then he typed up a letter to President Nixon, calling for him to resign "for crimes against humanity." He signed it, collected signatures from his teammates, and took it to Coach and asked him to sign it as well. Coach read the letter, and he was livid. "I can't sign this," he said, "and you're not sending it." But Walton sent it anyway. The relationship between Coach Wooden and Bill Walton was often rocky. But they loved each other, and they won championships together.

More than two decades after Walton graduated from UCLA, he and Coach made a journey together to Washington, DC. The two men were to be inducted together into the Academic All-America Hall of Fame. Soon after arriving, they visited the Lincoln Memorial together, and Walton was surprised and moved to hear his old coach recite the Gettysburg Address from memory. Then they walked over to the Vietnam Memorial, which Walton understandably called "the saddest place on Earth." There Coach recited—again, from memory—Grantland Rice's poem "Two Sides of War," a poem that closes with these lines:

> I've noticed nearly all the dead
> Were hardly more than boys.[4]

At that moment, Walton knew for certain what he'd always suspected: Coach Wooden felt the same way about the Vietnam War as he did. But Coach thought there was a right way and a wrong way to express opposition to the war. Getting jailed for protesting and writing letters demanding the president's resignation were, in John Wooden's view, the wrong way.

Walton vividly remembers a morning in late March 1975 when he picked up the morning newspaper and read that Coach Wooden had announced his impending retirement after UCLA's victory over Louisville in the semifinal game. Walton was in Portland, in his rookie season with the Trail Blazers. "It was out of nowhere," he later recalled. "I was shocked. Shocked. I was sad, disappointed, frustrated—because I knew how great and important he was. . . . What I was unaware of was that was just the beginning of a whole new life for him. So instead of just coaching twelve young men, he started coaching the world."[5]

After his retirement, Coach Wooden enjoyed a second career that included writing books, public speaking, and coaching at summer basketball camps. That second career lasted thirty-five years. And yes, John Wooden did, in fact, coach the world. And when Coach died, the whole world mourned.

Walton was one of a number of Coach Wooden's UCLA players who visited him at his deathbed. "I told him I loved him," Walton said, "and thanked him and apologized for all the consternation I caused in his life. What can you say to somebody who gave you everything? . . . When I left UCLA and joined the NBA, I became the highest-paid athlete in the history of sports, and my quality of life went *down*. That's how special it was to play for John Wooden. The sad part is that while we were doing it, we had no idea."[6]

A Conservative Man, yet Open to New Ideas

Whenever I visited Coach Wooden, I saw the stacks and stacks of mail he received. People would ask for his Pyramid of Success, and he would send them out by the dozens, by the hundreds. If people didn't think to include stamps, Coach would pay the postage himself. If you wrote and asked him for a word of advice or encouragement, he might send you a two- or three-page personal letter in his beautiful flowing penmanship. Coach always wrote back. I have one of his letters framed on my wall like a work of art—because it *is* a work of art.

When Coach and I returned to his condo after a meal, he always stopped to clear the messages on his answering machine. Most of the calls were from former players just checking in with their old coach. I often thought, *Here's a man who makes every day his masterpiece and who makes friendship a fine art.*

John Feinstein, the celebrated sports author, told me a story about Coach Wooden that speaks of the fatherly way Coach viewed everyone around him. One time when Feinstein was at the NCAA Final Four, he spotted Coach Wooden having breakfast in the hotel restaurant. Coach was in his late eighties at the time. Feinstein walked over and said, "Coach Wooden, I'm John Feinstein."

Coach smiled and shook his hand. "Oh yes, John. I certainly know you. I enjoy the work you do. What are you working on now?"

"I'm working with Red Auerbach on his memoirs," Feinstein said.

"Oh, Red Auerbach!" Coach said. "What a nice young man!"

Coach was born in 1910, and this "nice young man" was born in 1917. Red was in his eighties, as was Coach Wooden, yet Coach was totally sincere, not joking, when he called Red a "nice young man." To Coach, everyone must have seemed "young" compared to himself. Maybe that's why he was always teaching, always influencing, always sharing his wisdom with the people around him—including nice young people in their eighties.

Education speaker Dave Burgess saw Coach Wooden as a fascinating man who was, on the one hand, extremely conservative, even old-fashioned, but on the other hand, completely open to new ideas and new approaches. "Here's the conservative side of Coach Wooden," Burgess told me. "The most personal conversation I ever had with Coach was over a meal when I was a counselor at his camp. As we talked, he expressed concern because I had shown up at camp with an earring. He said, 'Dave, I don't think that earring fits your personality, your character.'

161

"I kind of shrugged off his concerns. He wasn't telling me to remove the earring, so I changed the subject, and I thought that would be the end of it. We talked some more, and near the end of our conversation, he said, 'Dave, do me a favor. I'd like you to wear a Band-Aid over that earring.'

"It was a powerful blow to have my hero, Coach Wooden, disapprove of my personal style."

I asked Burgess how he responded.

"I took the earring out."

Did he think Coach was being too rigid and inflexible?

"No, I think he was right. That earring *didn't* fit my character. I removed it and never wore an earring again."

Then Burgess told me another story—this time about how open-minded and accepting Coach Wooden could be.

"One day Coach saw me performing a dance style called popping or pop-lock for some of the campers. It's a street dance related to hip-hop in which you move your body in extreme ways, almost seeming to defy gravity. When Coach saw me doing this dance, he said he liked it because of the way it demonstrated balance. So he had me come up on the stage and perform it for the camp.

"I was surprised that he was so open to popping, because his taste in music was the Mills Brothers, not hip-hop. This was way out of his comfort zone. Yet he recognized the skill and importance of balance even in this urban dance form. He had an appreciation for it because of his emphasis on balance."

Just a few days into her first season as head coach of the women's basketball team at UCLA, Cori Close sat down with John Vallely, who played on Coach Wooden's 1969 and 1970 championship teams. Vallely told Close about the amazing impact this man, John Wooden, had made on his life. Close recalled, "He sat across from me and said: 'I've been married thirty-eight years because of lessons Coach Wooden taught me. I started three successful businesses because of what Coach Wooden taught me. I conquered cancer because of what Coach Wooden taught me. I survived the death of my twelve-year-old daughter because Coach Wooden *loved* me.'" That's what made Coach Wooden so special—not just that he taught but that he *loved*. "And for me," she concluded, "that's the standard."[7]

Who was this man who lived so competitively, walked so humbly, spoke so softly, taught so wisely, loved so unconditionally, and impacted so many lives at such a deep level?

Who Was John Wooden?

John Wooden was born on October 14, 1910, in the town of Hall, Indiana. His father, Joshua Hugh Wooden, and his mother, Roxie Anna Wooden, raised him in the virtues and values of the Bible. He had three brothers and two sisters (one sister died in infancy, the other at age two). In 1918, the Wooden family moved to a small farm near Centerton, Indiana (population eighty-six).

In 1924, hard times forced the Wooden family off the farm. They moved to Martinsville, Indiana (population forty-eight hundred). In 1926, John Wooden met the love of his life, Nell Riley, at a summertime carnival when he was fifteen and she was fourteen. They became high school sweethearts, and Nell was the only girl Wooden ever dated.

Wooden led the Martinsville High School Artesians to a state championship in 1927. He was selected all-state for three consecutive years. In 1928, Wooden and the Artesians again reached the Indiana high school championship, squaring off against Muncie. In the waning seconds of the game, Martinsville led 12-11 as Wooden took a shot, hoping to seal the win and give the Artesians back-to-back state titles. His shot bounced off the rim and was rebounded by the Muncie center, who launched a desperation shot. The ball sailed high into the rafters—and dropped down straight through the hoop. For years afterward, Wooden wished he could have that missed shot back. It was one of the few regrets of his life.

In the fall of 1928, Wooden enrolled at Purdue University in West Lafayette, Indiana, and played under Coach Ward "Piggy" Lambert. Wooden led Purdue to Big Ten championships in 1930 and 1932 and the national championship in 1932. At Purdue, he was nicknamed the "Indiana Rubber Man" because of his suicidal headlong dives after loose balls. He excelled in both athletics and academics and received the Big Ten Medal for Scholarship and Prowess, an honor he treasured for the rest of his life.

In August 1932, the day before Wooden was to marry Nell in a private ceremony in Indianapolis, a bank failure wiped out his savings—all the money he had set aside for their wedding. But they proceeded with the wedding anyway. After the ceremony, they attended a Mills Brothers concert at the Circle Theatre in Indianapolis—a memory Wooden always treasured.

In 1932, he accepted a position as English teacher, athletic director, and multi-sport coach at Dayton High School in Dayton, Kentucky. The Dayton Green Devils basketball team finished their first season under Coach Wooden with a 6-11 record—the only losing season of Wooden's coaching career.

In 1934, Wooden took a teaching-coaching job at South Bend Central High School in Indiana. On weekends, he barnstormed as a semipro basketball player. On that semipro team, he learned a new style of basketball that featured the fast break, unselfish passing, and coordinated teamwork that foreshadowed the kind of basketball he would later teach at UCLA.

That same year he began building his Pyramid of Success. He continued thinking about it, revising it, and testing it out in the laboratory of his life until 1948, when he felt he had perfected the Pyramid. It was a fourteen-year labor of love that became the foundation of his life and his approach to teaching basketball.

Against the advice of friends, he chose not to copyright the Pyramid, intending to make it freely available to all.

During the 1930s, Coach Wooden worked part-time as an editor for a book publisher. Meanwhile, he and Nell welcomed a daughter, Nan, and a son, Jim, to their family. In 1942, after the United States entered World War II, Wooden served as a lieutenant in the navy. After the war, he taught and coached at Indiana State Teachers College (now Indiana State University) in Terre Haute.

Coach Wooden's basketball squad won the 1947 Indiana Intercollegiate Conference title and an invitation to the National Association of Intercollegiate Basketball (NAIB) National Tournament in Kansas City. Wooden refused the invitation. The NAIB barred African-American players, and Coach had a black player, Clarence Walker, on his team. Such principled stands against racism were rare at the time, and Coach Wooden's vocal opposition led the NAIB to reverse its racist policy the following year.

In 1948, Wooden accepted an offer to coach the UCLA Bruins. His contract initially paid him $6,000 a year—near-poverty wages even in 1948. Coach later recalled, "My first four years at UCLA, I worked in the mornings at a dairy from six to noon. . . . I needed the money. . . . After all the trucks made their deliveries and came back, I would call in the next day's orders, sweep out the place, and head over the hill to UCLA."[8] After arriving on campus, he'd gather his assistants to mop the gym floor in preparation for the afternoon practice.

As the Bruins' coach, Wooden had immediate success, transforming a perennial loser into a 22-7 division champion in a single season. He continued coaching his teams to winning seasons year after year, establishing a record of sustained success. In the 1961–62 season, UCLA reached the NCAA Final Four for the first time, losing in the semifinal game after a debatable foul call. Two years later, Coach Wooden implemented the zone press defense, and

UCLA became a near-unstoppable force. The Bruins won ten national titles in twelve years, 1964 to 1975 (they fell short in 1966 and 1974).

In 1971, Coach Wooden and sports entrepreneur Max Shapiro started the John Wooden Basketball Fundamentals Camp, which continued into the mid-1980s. His wife, Nell, was a big part of the camp, always helping out with registration on the first day of camp. She was outgoing, gregarious, and protective of her husband. She prevented her overly trusting husband from being taken advantage of many times.

On March 21, 1985, John Wooden was at Nell's bedside, holding her hand, as she lost a courageous battle with cancer. After nearly fifty-three years of marriage, Coach was alone. He grieved deeply, and his friends and family worried he might never pull out of his depression.

Though he missed her every day, he eventually recovered his joy in life. On the twenty-first of each month, he visited her grave and wrote a love letter to her. He sealed each letter in an envelope, tied the letters with a ribbon, and kept them on her side of their bed. During one of my visits, he gave me a tour of his Encino condo, and I saw the stack of letters, neatly tied with a ribbon, on the bed.

Coach read his Bible daily and could quote many passages in the King James Version from memory. His daughter, Nan, told me that her father was constantly working to deepen his Christian character and his love for God.

For years, Coach kept a silver cross in his coat pocket. During games, he'd rub the cross between his fingers to dispel his nervous tension. The cross originally had the Greek letters alpha and omega etched into it. By the time he retired, he had worn the cross smooth.

Longtime UCLA radio announcer Fred Hessler once told me, "John Wooden tried harder than any man I've ever met to be like Jesus Christ." And Swen Nater told me, "One time while I was job hunting, I went to Coach for advice. He said, 'Swen, would you like me to pray about this with you? Let's ask God for his guidance in your life.' I never forgot that. He always honored God and the Bible. Talking to God was as natural to Coach as talking to his wife and kids."

In early June 2010, I was in the final stages of writing *Coach Wooden: The 7 Principles that Shaped His Life and Will Change Yours* (Revell, 2011) when my phone rang. It was Coach Wooden's daughter, Nan. "Pat," she said, "I'm calling to let you know that my brother, Jim, and I have put Daddy in the hospital. We don't expect him to come out."

"I'm so sorry, Nan," I said. "I'll be praying for Coach and for your family."

"Thank you. We're praying for him to go peacefully to be with Mother."

Nan and Jim had placed their father in the Ronald Reagan UCLA Medical Center. To keep the media and fans from intruding on Coach's final days, they checked him in under an assumed name. The doctors knew his identity, but some of the staff were in the dark.

One day a nurse entered Coach's room while Nan and Jim were there. She charted Coach's vital signs and double-checked the chart against his ID wristband. "Thank you, Mr. Adams," she said.

Coach said, "Who?"

"Mr. Adams. You're Gary Adams, aren't you?"

"No, I'm John Wooden."

The nurse smiled as if humoring him. "Okay—Mr. Wooden."

It was one of the few amusing moments Nan and Jim experienced in the closing days of their father's life.

Nan said that if you ever asked her father how he was doing in his faith or his character growth, he always said, "I'm working on it." One day Pastor Dudley Rutherford visited him at the hospital and asked, "Coach, you love the Lord, don't you?"

Coach softly responded, "I'm working on it."

Those words, Nan said, were the last words Coach Wooden spoke. On Friday evening, June 4, 2010, he went to be with Nell.

It was a sad day for those of us who knew him.

But for John Wooden, that day was his masterpiece.

9

Q&A with Coach Wooden

> While he is playing, the worst thing a player
> can think about in terms of concentration—and
> therefore of success—is losing. The next worst
> is winning.
>
> Coach John Wooden

What question would you like to ask Coach Wooden?

At his basketball camps, campers and parents and coaches had the rare privilege of asking Coach any question on any subject during the Q&A sessions following his Pyramid of Success talks. Craig Impelman and Greg Hayes had the foresight to videotape some of Coach Wooden's talks, including his Q&A sessions. He took questions from young and old, and they were the kinds of questions you and I would ask. His answers were revealing and insightful, and they have never appeared in any book or magazine before.

I culled through hours of video, unearthing this trove of wisdom from Coach Wooden. Let me share with you some of my favorite exchanges between Coach Wooden and the young (and not-so-young) people who came to his summer basketball camps to feast on his wisdom.

On the Pyramid of Success

After Coach gave a talk on his Pyramid of Success, one young camper asked, "How did you come up with the Pyramid of Success?"

"I came up with it," Coach Wooden replied, "because I didn't like the way people judged success. I wanted to come up with something to help me become a better teacher, something that would give young people a better goal to reach for. Instead of defining success as a higher mark in the classroom or winning an athletic competition, I wanted a standard that would help people become the best they are capable of becoming. I wanted young people to understand that success does not mean being better than someone else. It means being the best you can be."

Another camper asked, "If you could choose only one, what is the most important quality in the Pyramid of Success?"

Coach replied, "I would choose *all* of them! I couldn't choose one. They're all important. Every piece is important.

"It's like the players on a team: everybody's important. Some may seem more important than others, but they are all essential. Think of a team as a powerful automobile. Bill Walton might be a powerful engine. Another player might simply be a nut that holds the wheel onto the car. Is the engine more important than that nut? Yes, until the moment that nut comes loose and the wheel comes off the car. No matter how powerful your engine may be, if the car is missing a wheel because the nut fell off, that engine won't help you. So every part is essential.

"In the same way, every block of the Pyramid is essential. Take one block out, and the whole thing will fall apart. The Pyramid has served me well down through the years, so I'm hesitant to make any changes at this point."

One camper said he had a hard time dealing with criticism from other people.

Coach Wooden replied, "That's where the Pyramid can help you. When you build these traits into your life, criticism won't hurt so badly. Your enthusiasm will keep you focused on what matters. Your self-control will keep you from losing your temper. Your confidence will shield you. When you build these qualities into your life, the things people say can't hurt you as much.

"Wise people react the same way to both praise and criticism: they let it roll off them. Neither praise nor criticism should ever change you. Neither praise nor criticism should make you feel any different from before. If you feel good because you did well, there's nothing wrong with accepting awards for that. But you have to learn to accept criticism as well.

"Wise people react the same way to both praise and criticism: they let it roll off them."

"Criticism, for the most part, is intended to help you become a better person. This is especially true of the criticism you receive from your coaches or your parents. They want you to become a better person. So don't be carried away with either praise or criticism. Yes, you're going to enjoy praise more than criticism—that's only natural. But try to keep an even keel."

Another camper asked, "Why did you put friendship on the Pyramid?"

Coach said, "Because friendship is so important. Our ability to work with others is the key to teamwork. If you have a close friendship with somebody, and they with you, then together you can accomplish so much more than you ever could alone. There's nothing like having good friends. Your life should consist of faith, family, and friends, in that order. And remember, you have to *be* a friend in order to *have* a friend."

A very young camper asked, "How do you know all these things?"

A glint of amusement sparkled in Coach Wooden's eyes, but he treated the boy's question with seriousness. "I'll tell you," he said. "At different times, something would come up in my life that made me realize that this or that character trait was important. I realized that certain traits are essential to a successful life. I began building this Pyramid in 1934, and I completed it in 1948, and it has helped me through all the years since then."

Another camper asked, "What is the most successful thing in your life? Is it the Pyramid of Success?"

"My family is the most successful thing in my life," Coach said. "My children and my grandchildren and my thirteen great-grandchildren. But of anything that I personally developed, the Pyramid has had more effect than anything else. For forty years or more, I've sent out more than two thousand copies of the Pyramid every year. I never imagined this would happen when I began building the Pyramid. It's pleasing to me that people have found it helpful. That makes me feel good."

On Coach Wooden's Life and Personal Goals

A young camper asked, "Where did you come from?"

"I came from Hoosier-land," Coach said, "the great state of Indiana, and oh, what a beautiful state! Brown County, Indiana. There's an artists' colony there, because you have the lovely winter scenes, the spring scenes, the summer scenes, and that beautiful autumn. Oh, it's a wonderful state. Yes, it is."

An elementary-school camper asked, "When did you start to play basketball?"

"When I was about your size," Coach said. "I was on a grade-school team, and I started to play at school. I wanted to play at home too, so my dad knocked the bottom out of a tomato basket and tacked it up on the barn door. My mother made a basketball out of a cotton sock stuffed with rags, and she sewed it up to make it as round as possible. That was our first basketball. My brothers and I played, and we had a lot of fun. That's how I started playing basketball. Everybody is crazy about basketball in Indiana."

Another camper asked, "Did you ever get hurt as a player?"

"Yes," Coach said, "but never very seriously. My second-to-last year at Purdue, I had a severe thigh injury that curtailed my playing ability for a while, but I recovered. I played a year after that injury, but I didn't play as well. And I knew it was time to get out. And there were various injuries, minor injuries, like having a finger dislocated and so forth. And I got my nose broken two times. A few things. But all in all, the good Lord looked out for me pretty good."

One young camper asked, "When you were little, did you want to grow up to be a coach?"

"No, I didn't," Coach replied. "I had no aspirations to be a coach even when I graduated from high school. I entered Purdue University to become a civil engineer. But I didn't know that to get a degree in civil engineering, I had to go to civil camp every summer, and I didn't have the means to do that. There were no athletic scholarships in my day, and my parents didn't have the finances to put me through college, so I had to work in the summertime to earn money for school. That meant I had to drop my idea of becoming a civil engineer.

"I changed my major to liberal arts. Eventually, I knew I would be a teacher. After I graduated from Purdue, I taught English in high school and became a teacher of sports. At Indiana State, I taught English, baseball, basketball, and tennis. At UCLA, I taught only basketball."

Another camper asked, "Did you like teaching?"

Coach grinned broadly. "I did! I love to work with young people, and I've had a wonderful relationship with my students. I still keep in touch with many of my students to this day. Two years ago, I went back to Indiana and went to the school where I taught in the 1930s, and there was a surprise for me: twenty-six young men who had played for me in the 1930s and early 1940s, ranging in age from eighty to eighty-eight, were there to greet me. It was fun. In teaching, you establish a very close relationship with the young people under your supervision."

A teenage camper asked, "Is it true that you had only three rules for your players?"

"Oh, at one time I had a lot of rules and a few suggestions," Coach said. "Then I changed to having a few rules and a lot of suggestions. I ended up with three rules, and I required very definitely that we stick to those three rules as a team.

> *"At one time I had a lot of rules and a few suggestions," Coach said. "Then I changed to having a few rules and a lot of suggestions."*

"Rule 1 is 'Everyone must be on time for everything.' You must be on time to your classes, be on time to the table, be on time to practice, be on time for everything. It's so important to be on time. I'm sort of a nut about being prompt and on time.

"Rule 2 is 'Never use profanity.' Keep your speech clean. I once dismissed a player from my practice for the day because he used profanity. I required him to sit on the bench.

"Rule 3 is 'Never criticize a teammate.' That's my job, that's the role of the teacher, not the role of the student. As coach, it was my job to criticize a player's performance. I'm paid to do it. We were paid pitifully poor, but we were paid to do it. Of course, coaches are now paid more in one year than I was paid in forty years of teaching, but times change. I also used to be able to buy six hamburgers for a quarter."

Another teenage camper asked, "What is it like being in the Hall of Fame?"

"It's nice," Coach said, "but it's important to remember the people who made it possible. I wouldn't be in the Hall of Fame as a coach if I hadn't had the good fortune to have a lot of great players to coach. So it's a nice honor to be selected, but let's not get carried away."

One of the camp coaches asked, "Did you gain most of your knowledge of the game by playing at Purdue or through trial and error as a young coach?"

"Well," Coach said, "I hope I was learning more and more from year to year as a player and later as a coach. But my basic philosophy of the game, which was inculcated in my Pyramid of Success, is this: Get your team into the best possible physical condition. Teach your players to execute the fundamentals, not only properly but quickly. Teach them to play together as a team. All of that came primarily from my college coach, Ward 'Piggy' Lambert. In retrospect, I can see that he was ahead of his time—a great coach, a great individual, a man of extremely high principles. And I learned more from him than from any other one individual. He shaped my basic philosophy of the game and my philosophy of coaching.

"From the experience I gained coaching, I learned not to expect the same level of ability and performance from all my players. I learned that you cannot treat everybody the same. They are all different. You must treat each player as an individual. If you treat them all alike, you are actually showing partiality. I've heard people say, 'Oh, you're showing partiality by treating your players differently.' Oh no, if you treat everybody alike, you'll indulge some players and slight others. You must treat each player as an individual. You've got to give every player the treatment he has earned and deserves. I learned these principles by experience, but I learned my basic philosophy of coaching from my coach at Purdue.

"Coach Lambert inspired me to build my life on a foundation of principles. He, more than any other person in my life, inspired the ideas that form the heart of the Pyramid of Success. He is responsible for motivating me to build the Pyramid, for teaching me to execute the fundamentals properly but quickly, and for showing me how to teach my players a simple system that enables them to play together as a team."

A girl camper asked, "Were you ever offered coaching jobs in the NBA?"

"Yes," Coach Wooden said, "on five different occasions. The Lakers, the Clippers, the Bulls, the Pacers, and the Bucks all offered me coaching jobs. I was tempted. The money they offered was tempting, but I don't care for the way the game is played in the NBA. I think there's too much showmanship in the NBA—too much focus on individual play. Also, I would not have wanted to travel that much. There are so many road games. My wife wouldn't have liked that either.

"If you get your heart set on money, you set yourself up for trouble. True happiness comes from things that can't be taken away from you. Material things eventually go away."

"At the professional level, the coach is not really in charge. An outstanding player can get the coach dismissed. It has happened in many cases I could mention. The only thing that would be enticing at all is the money they pay you, but if you get your heart set on money, you set yourself up for trouble. True happiness comes from things that can't be taken away from you. Material things eventually go away."

Another girl camper asked, "Why did you retire?"

Coach grinned. "Because I was getting old!" he said. "And there were other reasons. My dear wife's health wasn't good. And she was worried about my health, and she wanted us to spend more time together. I thought it was time to get out."

On Coach Wooden's Years at UCLA

One coach asked, "Of all the players you have coached, who would be your all-time starting five?"

Coach laughed. "Oh my! What a question! Let me ask you something. Do you have children? You don't? Well, then, that won't work. I was going to ask you which of your children you like the most. No, I couldn't name five favorite players. I've been asked that question a number of times, but I couldn't choose.

"I will sometimes say this: I have never had a more valuable player than Lewis Alcindor. You know him as Kareem Abdul-Jabbar. He caused the opposition more trouble when he tended the court. And Bill Walton was perhaps an even better player. I've often said that I've never had a more spirited player than Dave Meyers, who was a tremendous leader for us in our last national championship. Keith Erickson and Gail Goodrich played with great tenacity and intensity. I've probably never had a smarter player than Mike Warren, and I probably never had a more physically talented player at forward than Sidney Wicks. And I never had a better all-around player at both ends of the floor than Keith Wilkes. Keith was an outstanding student, a gentleman in every way, and a wonderful basketball player who understood that championships are usually won through defense. He was a great defensive player.

"I may go out on a limb and make statements like that, but to pick an all-time starting five, that I could never do. It was always the team that won championships, not individual players."

Another coach asked, "Have you stayed in touch with many of the players you coached over the years?"

"Oh yes," Coach said. "I've been close with most of them through the years. I have breakfast fairly regularly now with a number of them. Most of my players, fortunately, have stayed in Southern California. And I regularly see Mike Warren, Kenny Washington, Andy Hill, Lynn Shackelford, Keith Erickson, and many others. I talk four times a week to Bill Walton. No, I shouldn't say that. I *listen* to Bill Walton.

"And there are many others, many who have not always been in the limelight. But I know pretty well where most of my players are today. And at the dedication of the floor at Pauley Pavilion a few years ago, when they named it the Nell and John Wooden Court, many of my players were on hand for the ceremony."

A woman said, "Coach, you didn't often call time-outs, but you would sometimes call a time-out when your team was behind in the fourth quarter, and you'd talk to your players. What did you say to them in the huddle?"

Coach laughed. "I'd say, 'Go out there and score! And score in a hurry!' Actually, what I told them would depend on the situation. If we're behind and seconds matter, we're going to set up a play, one of a number of plays we keep handy for emergency situations. It depends on the players you have and the mix of talents and abilities they possess. You might want to tell them something to increase their intensity and focus. Or you might want to tell them something that would relax them and keep them loose. You don't want them to lose their composure. You don't want them to act hastily and make mistakes. I would often explain again, 'Be quick but don't hurry.' What I would say would depend on many variables."

A camper said, "Coach Wooden, we watched a tape of you coaching the UCLA team, and you never yelled at your players. One of your players said you never asked them to go out and win the game. Why weren't you harder on your players?"

Coach replied, "I believe that outscoring your opponent doesn't necessarily make you a success. True success is making the effort and doing the best of which you are capable. That's the important thing. The score is not the important thing. I always wanted the score to be a by-product of our players doing their best.

"Yes, we worked hard. But I didn't believe in driving my players to be better than their opponents. I didn't like the dictator approach. I believe in motivating my players to do the best of which they are capable. I preferred the leader approach, not the dictator approach. But I worked my players hard. I expected a lot of them. We started practice on time, but we also quit on time. It was as important to quit on time as it was to start on time."

A teenage camper said, "Were you aware of the problems in society when you were coaching at UCLA? The civil rights marches, Vietnam, Watergate? Did those social issues affect your coaching?"

Coach said, "I was well aware of the problems going on in our country. Those were turbulent times. And what is going on in society in any era is always more important than what is going on in a college athletic program. There are always problems in society. When I first came to UCLA, it was shortly after the end of World War II. You are never without problems.

"When coaches today tell me that things are tougher now, that I coached in a much simpler era, I say they're crazy. There are always problems and always have been. And you have to cope with problems, whatever the problems are for that particular time. If you don't face problems squarely, they can come back and bite you."

A camper asked, "What was your main goal when you were coaching?"

"The first thing I wanted to get across to my players," Coach said, "is that they were at UCLA to get an education. I was more proud of the fact that all of my players graduated and got their degrees than all the championships. Most of my players have done well in their chosen profession. A great number of my players went on to play professional basketball in the NBA, and they did very well. More than thirty of my players went on to become attorneys, eight went on to become ministers, ten or more became doctors, a great number of them went on to become teachers or

> *"True success is making the effort and doing the best of which you are capable. That's the important thing."*

businessmen, or they found success in other professions. My first obligation was to encourage them to get an education. And we were successful in achieving that goal."

A camper asked, "What was the most memorable game you ever coached?"

"I'm inclined to say, the last game I coached," Coach said, "because then I don't have to think back so far. But seriously, we were not favored to win my last game, which was the national championship in 1975. We were up against a big, powerful University of Kentucky team. Winning the last game of my career was memorable, because our team overcame the odds. My players listened well. I was very proud of that team, and I enjoyed teaching them.

"Now, the *least* memorable game I ever had—or at least, the game I would most like to forget—was the year before that when we lost to North Carolina State in double overtime in the semifinals. I'd *really* like to forget that one, but I can't. The alumni won't let me forget it."

Dave Meyers, a former UCLA player who coached at the camps, said, "Coach Wooden, did your players ever get a swelled head? Did they ever think they were too important to pick up their towel when they showered? Did your players treat others with respect?"

"Well, sometimes they came into the program with swelled heads," Coach replied, "but they weren't that way when they left. Every year throughout my time at UCLA, the custodians at the schools we played would tell me, 'Your players leave the dressing room cleaner and neater than any other visiting team.' I didn't see any reason for our players to leave towels all over the floor. I told them, 'The manager is not your servant. He's there to help, but he's not there to clean up after you and do what you should do.' I insisted on the players being respectful and courteous and never thinking more of themselves than they ought to. I think that element of self-discipline made them better basketball players and better people.

"I insisted on courtesy to waitresses, courtesy to flight attendants, and courtesy to custodians. I think it's important that you, as campers, pick up after yourselves. When you're at home, keep your room clean. Help your parents around the house. Volunteer to do chores. Don't expect your mom to be your servant. Find ways to serve your mom and dad."

A camper asked, "How many championship rings do you have?"

"I don't have any rings," Coach said. "I gave them all away to my children and grandchildren."

On Basketball and the Art of Coaching

A coach asked, "What's the greatest attribute a coach needs to be successful?"

Coach Wooden said, "It's difficult to single out one attribute. But a coach certainly needs patience, a lot of patience. You must not expect too much too soon. This is true in teaching almost any subject, and it's no less true in coaching basketball. But there are many other things that are important, so I hesitate to single out one quality as *the* most important. But you asked for one attribute, and patience certainly is an important one.

"In addition, you must have a knowledge of your subject. And that's not enough. You must have the ability to communicate your knowledge to your players. When I was teaching basketball, I asked myself, 'Who knows more about the game of basketball than any other coach I know?' And I went to him on occasion for advice about certain things. He not only transmitted his knowledge to me but also helped me understand how to transmit that knowledge to my own players. It's a very poor coach who knows the game well but is not a good teacher. My coach at Purdue was a very good coach and a very good teacher, and I liked to talk to him about all aspects of the game."

A camper asked, "Which did you like better—playing or coaching?"

"When I played," Coach said, "I liked playing better. When I coached, I liked coaching better. And I enjoyed coaching much more when I had better players. I was often asked, 'Which opposing coaches gave you the most trouble?' My answer has always been, 'The ones that had the best players.'"

A camper asked, "What was the hardest part for you about being a coach?"

"The most difficult part, from a coaching point of view," Coach said, "was selecting players and cutting players. I found it very difficult, especially when I was coaching in high school. I'd have a lot of players try out for the team, and I'd have to cut it down to, say, twelve players. That was tough, having to tell some players they didn't make the team. Another difficult part is selecting who is going to start. I had players who were probably more valuable than starters, but they didn't get to start. And everybody wants to start. Those are the most difficult decisions a coach has to make."

A ten-year-old camper asked, "When you lost games, were you upset?"

"Disappointed more than upset," Coach said. "I would be more disappointed when I felt the team that outscored us was not as good as we were. And you have to be realistic: sometimes the other guy is just better. To lose to someone who is simply better, I wouldn't be upset. I would always be disappointed, but I would try not to be upset. I might be upset with an individual player who had not prepared himself as he should have. That's always disappointing."

One young camper identified himself as John, prompting John Wooden to say, "That's a good name!" The camper asked, "Did losing a game make you work harder the next week?"

"I hope not," Coach replied. "I hope I always worked as hard as I could. You can't work harder than that."

Another camper asked, "Did you ever make a bad student into a good student?"

"No," Coach Wooden said. "But did I help a struggling student become a better student? Goodness gracious, yes. If they wanted to play on my team, they had to become better students."

Dave Meyers asked, "If you could change three things about the game of basketball as it is played today, what would you change?"

Without hesitation, Coach said, "First, I would eliminate the dunk. I think it has brought on too much showmanship. And whenever you focus on showmanship, you take away from team play. I don't like sacrificing teamwork for showmanship.

"Second, I would move the three-point goal back. I think it's too short.

"Third, I'm not so sure I wouldn't prefer the international rules as far as the lane is concerned. I think that might make the game a little better. But that's only one person's opinion.

"I should point out that David Meyers asked that question. He won't tell you, but on the last team I coached, in the 1974–75 season, he was the leading scorer on the team. He won't tell you that, but I will. And he has reminded me many times that if I had played him more, he would have been the leading scorer for much longer than that."

A camper asked, "Who was your favorite player on your teams?"

Coach replied, "A coach must not have favorites. That's one thing you must not have. That doesn't mean you're going to like them all the same. A great coach by the name of Alonzo Stagg said, 'I never had a player I didn't love.' I'd like to be like that. But he also said, 'I had a lot I didn't like.' And you can love a player without liking him. You can even love people you don't respect. But you must not have favorites. You must not treat players differently because you like one more than you like the other. You don't always treat them exactly the same, but if you treat them differently, it must not be because one is your favorite and the other is not."

A girl camper asked, "Have you ever coached girls' basketball?"

"Only in camps like this one," Coach replied. "Girls' basketball camps are a lot of fun, and I think the best basketball today—the purest game, the simple game of basketball—is played by the better girls' basketball teams. They play below the rim instead of above the rim. They are fundamentally very sound. And technically, they play the game on a better level than the men. They're not as strong physically and can't do some of the things that the men do, but from a technical point of view, they play the purest game. I enjoy watching women's basketball."

Another girl asked, "Do you think you could still make a basket?"

Coach smiled and said, "Well, if I got close enough I could!"

On Faith and Character

A young camper asked, "What is your favorite book?"

"My favorite book? The Bible."

A parent asked, "Was there a particular experience in your life that brought you to Christ?"

"No," Coach said, "not one individual experience. I think it was a gradual process. I accepted Christ when I was a junior in high school because of Nellie. She was the only girl I ever dated. I was married to her for fifty-three years before she passed away. She wanted us to be baptized together, and we were.

"But there was a gradual process in which, at some point, that decision became real to me and central to my life. I can't point to the exact moment. I'm sure that moment came later than it should have, but I'm glad it eventually came."

Another adult said, "Coach, I've always been impressed by your composure on the sidelines during the games. Did you pretty much know you were going to win, based on how your teams had prepared during the week?"

"No," Coach said. "You never know beforehand if you're going to win. But you must prepare your players to the best of your ability so that they will execute to the best of their ability. Then you hope you're better prepared than the other team.

"As far as my composure during games, I looked at it this way: I tried to teach my players that if they lose their self-control, if they let their emotions take over, they are going to be outplayed. I felt that if I'm teaching self-control to my players, they have a right to expect self-control from me. So I made a special effort to keep my emotions under control.

"I never got off my seat while the clock was running. Time-outs, yes. When the clock stopped, I would get up. And I barbered the officials. I never called them names, I never swore, but I will confess that I sometimes said things I'm a little ashamed of today.

"There was one official in one game who made a horrible call. It happened to be against us. He made horrible calls against the other team too, but I didn't mind those. I did object when he made a bad call against us. As he ran past our bench, I called out, 'That was a horrible call, Lou!' He just grinned and said, 'They liked it at the other end!' Well, that was funny, so I couldn't get mad at him.

"The point is that when you have players under your supervision, if you are teaching them how to behave, then you'd better act in accordance with what you're teaching. The concepts you teach will come across more strongly through your actions than through your words.

"Young people, I know it's not easy for you to sit here and listen to an old man talk. We've talked about a lot of things, some of which you may not understand, but in time you will. Now work hard, and don't try to be better than somebody else. Simply try to be the best you can be. If you do that, you'll be a success."

Epilogue

Coach Wooden's Masterpiece

Seek opportunities to show you care. The smallest gestures often make the biggest difference.

Coach John Wooden

Craig Impelman is married to Coach Wooden's granddaughter
Christy. Impelman told me a story that sums up Coach Wooden
far better than any words of mine.

"Coach Wooden had been coming to my camps every year for
about thirty-five years. By this time, he was ninety-six or ninety-
seven. He had always been so generous in volunteering to come
speak to the campers. My wife and I had discussed Papa's involve-
ment in my camps, and we knew he'd never refuse a request. But
we worried about his health and strength, and we decided this
would be the last year we asked.

"The camp was at Ocean View High School in Huntington
Beach. The school has a big auditorium, but that year it was being
remodeled. We needed a different place where Coach could speak

187

to the campers. My wife gave me specific instructions: 'I don't want you to come up with some amphitheater in the hot sun. Make sure it's a comfortable, air-conditioned place.'

"I said, 'I'll take care of it.' But, of course, I waited until the last minute.

"The week of the camp rolled around, and it was Monday. I toured the campus with Jim Harris, the coach at the school, looking for a big enough room for Coach's talk, but every room Jim showed me was too small. He even showed me the amphitheater outside. I said, 'Coach, I can't do that. Christy told me we can't have Coach speaking out in the heat.'

"I was stuck. I didn't know what to do. Then Jim pointed to an old Baptist church across the street. He said, 'Maybe you can talk to the church about having Coach speak there.'

"I thought, *The pastor of that church won't want to let a bunch of six- to fourteen-year-olds use the church sanctuary for a basketball camp.* But I was out of options, so we got in Jim's car. I gave Jim some bad instructions, and we turned the wrong way and ended up going around a long block before we got back to the church. Finally, with the blessing of providence, we pulled up at the church just as the pastor was walking out of his office.

"I jumped out of the car and said, 'Pastor!' I ran over to him and introduced myself. I explained our circumstances and said we needed a place where our guest speaker could talk to the kids from our camp. Could we use the church?

"He looked skeptical, and I thought he was about to say no. Then I said, 'Our speaker is Coach John Wooden. This will be his last time speaking to a basketball camp.'

"The pastor's eyes lit up, and he said something I'll never forget: 'I can't think of any more appropriate use for our church than having John Wooden talk to the youth of our community. If it's Coach Wooden, that will be just fine.'

"So on Friday, Coach Wooden stepped up to the pulpit and gave one of the best talks ever on the Pyramid of Success, followed by a wonderful question-and-answer session. The kids sat in rapt attention as basketball's greatest coach talked to them about good values and the real meaning of success.

"God timed it all just right—even my last-minute attempt to find an auditorium and my wrong-turn directions to Jim."

Yes, the timing was right, and the pastor said it well: there's no better place for the next generation to be than sitting at the feet of John Wooden listening to him talk about good character and good values.

Coach Wooden isn't with us anymore, but he left us his words, his passion, and his legacy of teaching and influencing future generations of young people. Now it's up to you and me to carry on his work, to use our influence, to teach our children and our children's children. I can't think of any more appropriate use for our lives than to follow Coach Wooden's example, to live as he lived, to help others, and to teach and coach and mentor the next generation.

That's how Coach Wooden lived each day. That's how he made each day his masterpiece.

I Saw Love Once
by Swen Nater

I saw love once; I saw it clear.
It had no leash; it had no fear.

It gave itself without a thought.
No reservation had it bought.

It seemed so free to demonstrate.
It seemed obsessed to orchestrate

A symphony, designed to feed,
Composed to lift the one in need.

Concern for others was its goal,
No matter what would be the toll.

It's strange just how much care it stores,
To recognize its neighbor's sores,

And doesn't rest until the day,
It's helped to take those sores away.

Its joy retains and does not run,
Until the blessing's job is done.

I saw love once; 'twas not pretend.
He was my coach; he is my friend.

for Coach Wooden on Christmas 1998
Used by permission.

191

Notes

Introduction

1. Greg Hayes, *Camp with Coach Wooden: Shoes and Socks, the Pyramid, and "A Little Chap"* (Santa Clarita, CA: Greg Hayes, 2015), 171.

Chapter 1 More than a Basketball Camp

1. Jim Caviezel, "John Wooden's Lessons Helped Me in Hollywood," *Indianapolis Star*, September 8, 2014, http://www.indystar.com/story/opinion/2014/09/08/jim-caviezel-john-woodens-lessons-helped-hollywood/15278147/; Angela Dawson, "Jim Caviezel Standing 'Tall' as Coach in Football Movie," FrontRowFeatures.com, August 19, 2014, http://frontrowfeatures.com/features/film-features/jim-caviezel-standing-tall-as-coach-in-football-movie-8778.html.
2. Dick Kazan, "A Personal Memory of Coach John Wooden," KazanToday.com, June 22, 2010, http://www.kazantoday.com/WeeklyArticles/john-wooden.html.
3. Hayes, *Camp with Coach Wooden*, 61.
4. Ibid., 161.

Chapter 2 Success Is in the Details

1. Kurt Helin, "Memories and Lessons from the John Wooden Basketball Camp," NBCSports.com, June 5, 2010, http://nba.nbcsports.com/2010/06/05/memories-and-lessons-from-the-john-wooden-basketball-camp/.
2. Hayes, *Camp with Coach Wooden*, 51.
3. John Wooden and Steve Jamison, *Wooden on Leadership: How to Create a Winning Organization* (New York: McGraw-Hill, 2005), 135–36.
4. John Wooden and Steve Jamison, *The Essential Wooden: A Lifetime of Lessons on Leaders and Leadership* (New York: McGraw-Hill, 2006), 72.
5. Alexander Wolff, "16 John Wooden," *Sports Illustrated*, September 19, 1994, https://www.si.com/vault/1994/09/19/132048/16-john-wooden.

6. Wooden and Jamison, *The Essential Wooden*, 65.
7. Billy Packer with Roland Lazenby, *Why We Win* (New York: Masters Press, 1999), 45.
8. André McCarter, "The Pyramid of Success," *Guideposts*, October 27, 2008, http://www.guideposts.org/inspirational-stories/inspiring-stories-ucla-coach-john-wooden.
9. André McCarter, "John Wooden's 'Ultimate Championship,' Part 3," Christian Broadcasting Network, June 4, 2011, http://www1.cbn.com/john-woodens-ultimate-championship-part-3.

Chapter 3 Be a Leader Who Builds Leaders

1. Don Yaeger, "Timeless Lessons from John Wooden, the Greatest Coach of All Time" ("Dale Brown: Three Secrets to Success"), Success.com, March 13, 2016, http://www.success.com/article/timeless-lessons-from-john-wooden-the-greatest-coach-of-all-time.
2. Hayes, *Camp with Coach Wooden*, 75.
3. Ibid., 40.
4. Ibid., 24.
5. Ibid., 41.
6. Ibid., 27–28.
7. Ronn Wyckoff, "Coach: A Coach's Family Influenced by John Wooden," Top-Basketball-Coaching.com, June 29, 2010, http://www.top-basketball-coaching.com/CoachWooden.
8. Don Yaeger, "Timeless Lessons from John Wooden, the Greatest Coach of All Time" ("Cori Close: It's about More than Trophies"), Success.com, March 13, 2016, http://www.success.com/article/timeless-lessons-from-john-wooden-the-greatest-coach-of-all-time.
9. Cecilia Meis, "Passing the Torch," *Success Magazine*, March 2017, 74–77.
10. Angela Lento, "Driving Coach Wooden," CollegeInsider.com, 2004, http://www.collegeinsider.com/angela/hawkins.html.

Chapter 4 Be a Teacher

1. Nathan Barber, "John Wooden Quotes on Teaching and Learning," The Next Generation of Educational Leadership, June 22, 2014, http://nextgenedu leaders.blogspot.com/2014/06/john-wooden-quotes-on-teaching-and.html.
2. Joe Moore, "Writing Doesn't Make You a Better Writer," *Kill Zone* (blog), July 13, 2014, https://killzoneblog.com/category/john-wooden.
3. Matt Lait and Mike Faneuff, "Summers with John Wooden," *Los Angeles Times*, June 13, 2010, http://articles.latimes.com/2010/jun/13/sports/la-sp-wooden-camp-20100613.

Chapter 5 Teach Wisdom, Not Winning

1. John Wooden and Steve Jamison, *Wooden's Complete Guide to Leadership* (New York: McGraw-Hill, 2011), 197–98.

2. Dan Steinberg, "John Wooden's Handwritten Letter to Gary Williams," *Washington Post*, January 17, 2014, https://www.washingtonpost.com/news/dc-sports-bog/wp/2014/01/17/john-woodens-handwritten-letter-to-gary-williams/?utm_term=.ca32973f34ba.

3. Lait and Faneuff, "Summers with John Wooden."

Chapter 6 Empower Your People

1. Neville L. Johnson, *The John Wooden Pyramid of Success* (Los Angeles: Cool Titles, 2003), 419.

2. Pat Williams, *How to Be Like Coach Wooden: Life Lessons from Basketball's Greatest Leader* (Deerfield Beach, FL: Health Communications, Inc., 2006), 15.

3. Tarik Trad, "UCLA Basketball Coach John Wooden: More than a Coach," Patheos.com, June 7, 2010, http://www.patheos.com/blogs/altmuslim/2010/06/more_than_a_coach/.

4. Steve Jamison, "Memory Wall," CoachWooden.com, http://www.coachwooden.com/memory-wall (some quotations paraphrased for clarity).

5. Ann Meyers Drysdale with Joni Ravenna, *You Let Some GIRL Beat You?* (Lake Forest, CA: Behler Publications, 2012), 137.

6. Kelly Schaefer with Michelle Weidenbenner, *Fractured Not Broken: A Memoir* (Leesburg, IN: Kelly Schaefer LLC with R. Publishing LLC, 2015), 105–7.

7. Ibid., 179.

Chapter 7 Strive for Competitive Greatness

1. Barbara Olenyik Morrow, *Hardwood Glory: A Life of John Wooden* (Indianapolis: Indiana Historical Society Press, 2014), 179; Robert Siegel, "John Wooden: An English Teacher Who Happened to Be a Hoops Legend," National Public Radio: All Things Considered, January 10, 2014, http://www.npr.org/2014/01/10/261435118/john-wooden-an-english-teacher-who-happened-to-be-a-hoops-legend.

2. Steve Bisheff, *John Wooden: An American Treasure* (Nashville: Cumberland House, 2004), 220.

3. Ibid.

4. Ibid.

5. Ibid., 221.

6. Clay Skipper, "The Thing Bill Walton Still Can't Forgive Himself For," GQ.com, March 26, 2016, http://www.gq.com/story/bill-walton-back-from-the-dead-interview.

7. Gary Adams, *Conversations with Coach Wooden* (Solana Beach, CA: Santa Monica Press, 2013), 187.

8. David Wharton and Chris Foster, "John Wooden's Words Live On in the Hearts of His Admirers," *Los Angeles Times*, June 6, 2010, http://articles.latimes.com/2010/jun/06/sports/la-sp-0606-john-wooden-20100606.

9. Ibid.

10. John Feinstein, *Last Dance: Behind the Scenes at the Final Four* (New York: Little, Brown, 2006), 81–82.

11. Hayes, *Camp with Coach Wooden*, 61.
12. Steve Laube, "In Memory of John Wooden," SteveLaube.com, June 5, 2010, https://stevelaube.com/in-memory-of-john-wooden/.
13. Matthew Snyder, "Great Momentum: Coach Cori Close Talks about a UCLA Team on the Verge of Greatness," SlamOnline.com, October 14, 2014, http://www.slamonline.com/college-hs/college/cori-close-ucla/.

Chapter 8 The Undiscovered Coach Wooden
1. Michael Mink, "John Wooden Stayed Consistent While Winning Huge," *Investor's Business Daily*, March 27, 2015, http://www.investors.com/news/manage ment/leaders-and-success/john-wooden-stayed-consistent-throughout/.
2. Wharton and Foster, "John Wooden's Words Live On in the Hearts of His Admirers."
3. Skipper, "The Thing Bill Walton Still Can't Forgive Himself For."
4. Nick Canepa, "Wooden-Walton Relationship Has a Lasting Impact," *San Diego Union-Tribune*, June 6, 2010, http://www.sandiegouniontribune.com/sdut -wooden-walton-relationship-has-a-lasting-impact-2010jun06-story.html.
5. Bryce Miller, "The 52: John Wooden Announces Retirement at Sports Arena," *San Diego Union-Tribune*, September 9, 2016, http://www.sandiego uniontribune.com/sdut-john-wooden-ucla-retirement-san-diego-final-four-2016 sep09-story.html.
6. Skipper, "The Thing Bill Walton Still Can't Forgive Himself For."
7. Howard Megdal, "UCLA Women's Coach Cori Close Follows John Wooden's Example," *New York Times*, November 16, 2016, https://www.nytimes.com/2016 /11/17/sports/ncaabasketball/ucla-women-cori-close-john-wooden.html?_r=1.
8. Brendan Prunty, *Basketball's Game Changers: Icons, Record Breakers, Rivalries, Scandals, and More* (Lanham, MD: Rowman & Littlefield, 2017), 16.

Pat Williams is senior vice president of the NBA's Orlando Magic. He has more than fifty-five years of professional sports experience, has written dozens of books, including the popular *Coach Wooden* and *It's Not Who You Know, It's Who You Are*, and is one of America's most sought-after motivational speakers. He lives in Florida. Find out more at www.patwilliams.com.

Jim Denney is the author of the Timebenders science-fantasy series for young readers (beginning with *Battle Before Time*), and such nonfiction titles as *Walt's Disneyland* and *Writing in Overdrive*. His collaborative titles include numerous books with Pat Williams, including *Coach Wooden*, *Coach Wooden's Greatest Secret*, and *The Sweet Spot for Success*.

CONNECT WITH PAT

We would love to hear from you. Please send your comments about this book to Pat Williams:

pwilliams@orlandomagic.com

Pat Williams
c/o Orlando Magic
8701 Maitland Summit Boulevard
Orlando, FL 32810

If you would like to set up a speaking engagement for Pat, please contact his assistant, Andrew Herdliska:
(407) 916-2401
aherdliska@orlandomagic.com

PATWILLIAMS.COM

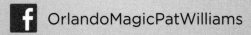 OrlandoMagicPatWilliams

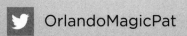 OrlandoMagicPat

LEGENDS AREN'T BORN.
They're MADE.

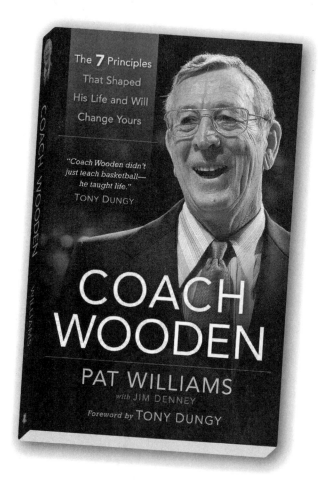

Based on seven principles given to Coach Wooden by his father,
this book helps the reader discover how to be successful and
a person of character and integrity.

COACH WOODEN
Knew the Long-Term Impact *of* Little Things DONE WELL

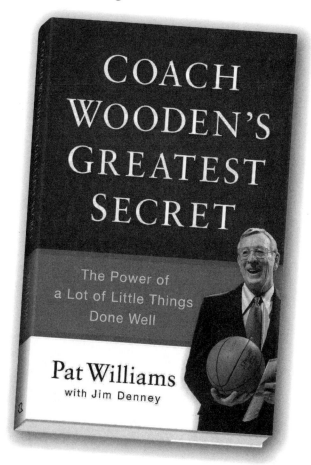

A motivational message filled with life-changing insights and memorable stories—Pat Williams shares why the secret to success in life depends on a lot of little things done well.

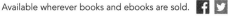

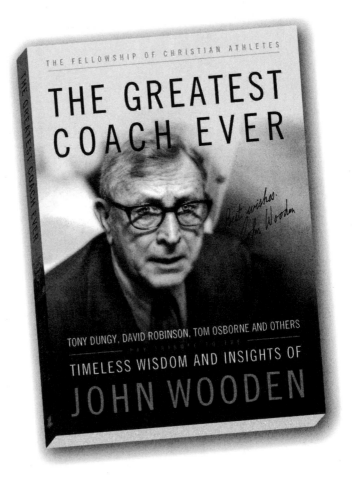

The Coach of the Century
Reveals His
SECRET TO SUCCESS

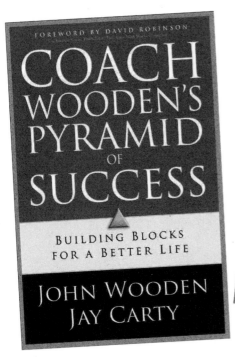

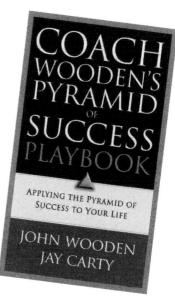

Go deeper with Coach Wooden
and the Pyramid of Success.

FIND SUCCESS WHERE YOUR
TALENT AND PASSIONS MEET

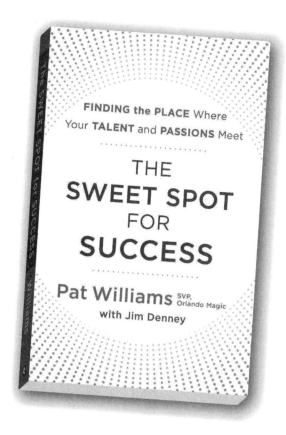

"Pat Williams's waste-no-time philosophy has informed my work ethic for decades. *The Sweet Spot for Success* distills all he's learned and put into practice. Pat lays it out in such a way that you can easily intersect your talent with your passion to discover your sweet spot in life. Now *that's* success!"

—**JERRY B. JENKINS,** novelist and biographer; founder, The Jerry Jenkins Writers Guild

Inspiration and Guidance for a Life of
INTEGRITY and EXCELLENCE

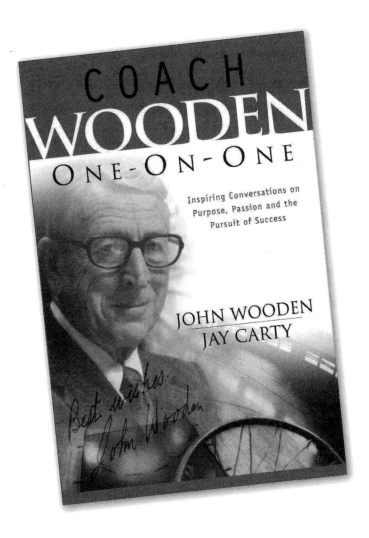